you&your
Jeep
Cherokee

you & your

Jeep
Cherokee

Dave Pollard Buying, enjoying, maintaining, modifying

First published in February 2005

Dave Pollard has asserted his right to
be identified as the author of this work.

British Library cataloguing-in-publication data:
A catalogue record for this book is available
from the British Library

Published by Haynes Publishing,
Sparkford, Yeovil, Somerset BA22 7JJ, UK

Tel: 01963 442030 Fax: 01963 440001
Int. tel: +44 1963 442030 Int. fax: +44 1963 440001
E-mail: sales@haynes.co.uk
Website: www.haynes.co.uk

ISBN 1 84425 137 3

Library of Congress catalog card no. 2004113001

Haynes North America, Inc.,
861 Lawrence Drive, Newbury Park,
California 91320, USA

Designed by G&M Designs Limited,
Raunds, Northamptonshire
Printed and bound in Great Britain by
J. H. Haynes & Co. Ltd, Sparkford

Contents

Acknowledgements

My thanks to all who have helped in the production of this book, notably Nick O'Donnell, Jackie Allard and Jo Ayers at Daimler Chrysler UK, Nigel at Westbury, the official Shrewsbury Jeep dealership, Elliot Dunmore at

EDM Jeep Specialists, and the many and various owners who have been patient while being quizzed about their cars and when being photographed. Unless otherwise credited, photos are from the author, Daimler Chrysler library and Nick Dimbleby.

Dave Pollard
December 2004

More than 60 years after the original, all Jeeps are instantly recognisable – even if that seven-slot grille is now chrome plated! (Nick Dimbleby)

Introduction

The history of Jeep started when it became clear that a world war was on the cards. The role of the Willys Jeep during the Second World War has been well documented and it is not gilding the lily to suggest that in many respects, it was pivotal to allied success. Since then, the company has seen many and various changes of ownership and has survived harsh economic conditions – not least due to oil crises through the years – to emerge triumphant in the 21st century as one of the world's major 4x4 players.

Certainly, the drivers of those 1940s utility machines would find it hard to imagine the level of luxury that is now offered (both in the Cherokee and the Grand Cherokee), but they would probably find it even more difficult to believe this has been achieved without sacrificing off-road abilities.

Something else to consider is that, despite the fact that we are now more than 60 years down the line, those war-time drivers would still recognise, say, the new Cherokee (Liberty in North America from 2001 model) from 50 yards away, because the company has managed to retain the trademark seven-slot grille. To achieve this, despite the restrictions placed on designers with regard to aerodynamics and safety, is quite amazing. The Jeep sales line reflects what its enthusiast owners already know: Jeep – there's only one.

Making Tracs – Jeep's various 4WD systems explained

All Cherokees (and Wranglers) come with four-wheel drive, but there are differences in application. All models have a low-ratio gearbox, which is essential for proper off-road driving, but this can also be useful day-to-day, for example, low-ratio reverse can be very handy when backing with a trailer or caravan.

For UK users, the reference to 'part-time' and 'full-time' 4WD modes can be a bit confusing. Part-time means that four-wheel drive (4WD) can only be engaged when truly necessary (snow and mud etc.) and that either there is no centre differential, or that where present, the centre diff is locked. As such it should be disengaged as soon as it is not required to avoid damage. Full-time 4WD means just that; the vehicle has four-wheel drive, all the time, not just when specifically selected.

Command-Trac

In normal on-road conditions, the drive goes solely to the rear wheels. For off-road use or driving in snow or other slippery conditions, selecting the Command-Trac option brings the front wheels into play. However, there is no central differential so using this for any length of time on metalled roads would result in axle 'wind-up' and, eventually, damage to the transmission.

Selec-Trac

With this system, the Jeep can run in four-wheel-drive mode all the time, although it is possible to select two-wheel drive mode if required, in theory at least to gain extra mpg. A central viscous differential is fitted and in normal, tarmac road conditions, around 90 per cent of the torque goes to the rear wheels. However, when wheel slippage is detected, torque is redistributed accordingly.

Quadra-Trac

This is a permanent 4WD system, made possible thanks to the fitment of a centre differential. No driver input is required to select 4WD.

Quadra-Drive

First seen on the 1999 Grand Cherokee this is a combination of the second-generation Quadra-Trac II transfer case and Vari–Lok progressive front and rear axle differentials. It gives permanent 4WD, and in normal driving conditions, most power is delivered to the rear wheels. However, if either rear wheel loses traction the speed variation will cause the gerotor pump to apply hydraulic pressure to a multi-disc clutch-pack sending power to the front axle. This works seamlessly and without any driver input being required. As usual, both low and high range gears are available.

Rewards and awards

Motoring magazines and organisations just love awards ceremonies and the guys at Jeep don't mind them either, as you'll see from this list of silverware collected over the years.

Year	Car	Magazine/Organisation	Award
1993	Cherokee	Caravan Club	All-terrain tow car of the year (1994)
1995	Grand Cherokee	4Wheel & Off Road (USA)	4x4 of the Year
1996	Grand Cherokee	Auto Express	4x4 of the Year
1996	Grand Cherokee	What Car?	4x4 of the Year
1997	Grand Cherokee	Auto Express	4x4 of the Year
1997	Grand Cherokee	What Car?	4x4 of the Year
1997	Grand Cherokee	Off Road and 4-Wheel Drive	Off-Roader of the Year
1998	Grand Cherokee	Auto Express	4x4 of the Year
1999	Grand Cherokee	What Car?	Best Off-Roader
1999	Grand Cherokee	Auto Express	Used 4x4 of the Year
1999	Grand Cherokee	Evening Gazette Group	Sports Utility & 4x4 of the Year
1999	Grand Cherokee	AA Journal	Best Off-Roader
1999	Grand Cherokee	Off Road and 4-Wheel Drive	4x4 of the Year (2000)
2000	Grand Cherokee	What Car?	Best Off-Roader
2000	Grand Cherokee	Top Gear	Best Off-Roader
2000	Grand Cherokee	Off Road and 4-Wheel Drive	Used 4x4 of the Year (luxury)
2000	Cherokee	Off Road and 4-Wheel Drive	Used 4x4 of the Year (overall)
2000	Cherokee	Off Road and 4-Wheel Drive	Best heavy-duty 4x4
2000	Grand Cherokee	Association of Scottish Motoring Writers	Leisure Car of the Year
2000	Grand Cherokee	Auto Express	Used 4x4 of the Year
2001	Cherokee	Off Road and 4-Wheel Drive	Used 4x4 of the Year (overall)
2001	Wrangler	Off Road and 4-Wheel Drive	Used 4x4 of the Year (lifestyle)
2001	Cherokee	AA/Association of Scottish Motoring Writers Scottish Car of The Year Awards	Best 4x4
2001	Grand Cherokee	4x4	4x4 of the Year (luxury)
2001	Wrangler	4x4	4x4 of the Year (overall and hardcore)
2002	Grand Cherokee	Used Car Buyer	Used 4x4 of the Year
2002	Cherokee	4x4	4x4 of the Year (compact)
2003	Cherokee	4x4	4x4 of the Year (mid size)
2004	Cherokee	4x4	4x4 of the Year (2005)

The 4x4 as an enemy of the people – the facts behind the political agendas

As this book was being prepared, there were moves afoot to start penalising owners of 4x4 vehicles; some were suggesting they should pay double the London congestion charge, others that they should be banned altogether from some places. Thankfully, there was a voice of reason, too, in the form of the RAC Foundation which questioned many of the premises on which certain allegations (usually to do with 'green' issues) were made.

Far from finding that all 4x4 vehicles are gas-guzzling, eco-unfriendly monsters, they discovered that some models were actually cleaner, greener, smaller, shorter and safer than many standard saloons and even people carriers. Quite predictably, especially with an election due, politicians of all hues were quick to dive on the bandwagon, regardless of the facts behind the case.

Edmund King, executive director of the RAC Foundation said: 'These suggestions are ludicrous. It is not the job of politicians to dictate what vehicles people should drive. Of course, motorists should choose vehicles that are the most suitable for the types of journeys and the goods or people that they carry. But there is great diversity within the range of 4x4s.

'In a democracy there is no place for politicians or the anti car brigade telling motorists what vehicle they may or may not drive. Perhaps this is more about the politics of envy rather than the politics of democracy.'

The Foundation contrasted some of the claims made by politicians with the realities in a bid to clarify the argument:

Environment

Claim: All 4x4s are bad for the environment.

Reality: The average CO_2 of a dual-purpose 4x4 is more than 12 per cent lower than most luxury saloons and on a par with emissions from executive and sports cars. Most vehicles sold in the 4x4 segment are diesel variants; they have better fuel consumption and emit less CO_2 than petrol models. Many manufacturers are also working to bring alternative fuel versions to market.

Size

Claim: All 4x4s are two-tonne monsters that take up more road space, so increasing congestion.

Reality: While often taller than other models, some of the most popular 4x4s are narrower and shorter than the average saloon car. In fact, if parents co-ordinate their school-runs using all available seats in their vehicles, the number of cars making the journey could actually be cut by using a 4x4. Research shows that 71 per cent of owners of a 4x4 model with three rows of seats regularly use them.

Safety

Claim: All 4x4s pose a threat to other road users and pedestrians, beyond that associated with normal saloon cars.

Reality: Improvements to front-end design of many 4x4s have resulted in them increasingly scoring well on pedestrian protection in EuroNCAP tests. Two models both scored two stars in recent NCAP tests; while the third best-selling 4x4 in Britain achieved an impressive three-star rating. There are many examples of models in other segments that perform less well than current 4x4 models.

Lifestyle

Claim: All 4x4s are an aspirational product driven by rich, urban women to do the shopping.

Reality: They may be chosen because of the capacity and storage they offer, their performance, driving position, style, safety or suitability for the environment in which they travel.

Mr King added: 'Drivers should, of course, think carefully before choosing a vehicle that fits their needs, their lifestyle, their family, their pocket and their environment and be responsible for how they use that vehicle in rural and urban conditions but critics of 4x4s seem to dwell on polarised stereotypes and massage figures to suit their arguments rather than look at the full range of vehicles available, their uses and their capabilities.'

Chapter One

Jeep History

Since it first entered popular parlance over half a century ago, the word 'Jeep' has been transformed from military standard-bearer of manoeuvrability and versatility to a byword for the ultimate in sporty four-wheel drive fun, style and capability. Can you think of another military weapon to start a new life of pleasure-giving to so many people? The Jeep story officially began in 1941 when Willys-Overland started making Jeeps in its Ohio, USA factory. An authentic and restored example in the Chrysler Jeep Imports UK collection, built in 1942, is one of those early vehicles.

However, it was three years earlier, in 1938, that the seeds of the Jeep were sown.

The US Army wanted to replace the motorcycle-sidecar combinations it used for messenger and advance reconnaissance duties, with a small, general-

Left: America, the home of rock and roll – and there's plenty of rocks here to give these Wranglers a good workout. (Nick Dimbleby)

Below: How it all started – this wartime MB Jeep has been restored and is now part of DaimlerChrysler's UK collection.

purpose vehicle. It let American motor manufacturers know what it was looking for and, following an official US Army request in 1940, three companies responded with prototype vehicles – Willys Overland's Quad, the American Bantam Car Company's Blitz Buggy, and the Ford Motor Company's GP.

Bantam delivered three prototypes to the Army in September 1939. Each weighed 1,275lb but, after thorough testing, were deemed useless. Willys-

Overland, meanwhile, put Delmar 'Barney' Roos, its vice-president of engineering, on the case, and he came up with sketches of what he called a 'mosquito' car. Col Rutherford, chief of the Planning Section of the General Staff, liked what he saw in December 1939, and Willys-Overland rapidly developed the concept into a light, manoeuvrable and powerful all-purpose vehicle capable of carrying troops as well as weapons. The Army was impressed.

Yet in June 1940, Army officers visited the Bantam factory to examine a second Bantam reconnaissance model. This time, it was considered too light and, again, rejected. However, when the Army, now losing patience, asked 135 manufacturers for quick delivery of 70 vehicles in July – weighing 1,300lb with a 660lb payload, an engine giving 85lb ft of torque, and an 80in wheelbase – Bantam was the only company that promised pilot car delivery in 49 days and total delivery in 75 days. Willys bid 75 days for delivery of the pilot and 120 days for total delivery. Bantam won the bid.

Barney Roos, though, had added a note to the unsuccessful Willys bid stating that 'no substantial vehicle' was possible at 1,300lb. He also explained this to Major H. J. Lawes, purchasing and contracting officer for Camp Holabird, and Lawes suggested Willys-Overland build its own pilot model to prove it. Ford, another bid loser, was also given this tip-off as the Government wanted the choice of as many designs as possible.

Roos built his vehicle as sturdily as he could, while keeping light weight in mind. Then, in September 1940, Bantam designer Karl Probst delivered a prototype called the 'Blitz Buggy' to Camp Holabird. Willys engineers, including Roos, could hardly believe its agility, stamina and compactness, and returned to Toledo to spur on their own design team.

Two Willys-Overland vehicles were subsequently delivered on 11 November 1940 to Army officials at Camp Holabird. Named 'Quad', they had selectable two or four-wheel drive, and one boasted four-wheel steering. The Army was impressed, but Bantam was apoplectic because the Quad looked almost identical to Probst's Blitz Buggy, and claimed Willys had simply copied design ideas. Perhaps this wasn't surprising: the Army had given them free access to Bantam blueprints, after all – in the name of expediency, of course!

This is an Air Force Dispatcher version of the CJ-5. Again, the hard-top does nothing for the looks, but the massively rounded bonnet/lamp design was to become a trademark for many years. Incredibly, this model lasted in its basic format from 1954 until 1986, albeit with many and various updates along the way and with designations up to CJ-8 Scrambler.

Bantam, Willys and Ford prototypes did differ. The 2,030lb Bantam vehicle bust the original 1,300lb weight stipulation, but it was still lighter than the 2,400lb Willys. However, the Willys was the only one to meet the Army's power specifications.

In fact, the Willys's 105lb ft of torque from its gutsy, tried-and-trusted 'Go Devil' engine not only exceeded the requirement, it dwarfed Bantam's 83lb ft and Ford's 85lb ft from as-yet unproven motors.

With prototypes from the three companies in hand, the Army ordered 4,500 vehicles, 1,500 from each company, to test them in the field. Acknowledging that 1,300lb was unrealistic, the new weight requirement was 2,160lb.

Roos and his team set about lightening the Quad by completely dismantling the vehicle and re-assembling it – while evaluating each part to see if a lighter material could be substituted. They trimmed extra thread off bolts and removed other surplus metal until the Jeep was just 7oz off its target weight.

Delivery of the 4,500 models began in June 1941, and the Army, perhaps inevitably, decided to standardise on one basic design. At last, the Willys set the standard, with modifications to incorporate some

features of the Ford and Bantam. In July 1941, Willys then underbid Bantam and Ford in an all-or-nothing contract for 16,000 vehicles at a rate of 125 per day. Later that year, the Quartermaster Corps of the Army, pressed for other sources of supply, and requested Willys-Overland turn over designs of its vehicle to Ford to boost production.

During the Second World War, Willys and Ford built some 600,000 Jeeps, with Willys-Overland supplying more than 368,000 … and tiny Bantam just 2,675, most of which were given to Britain and the Soviet Union under the Lend-Lease Act. Bantam production ceased just before Japan's attack on Pearl Harbor.

As production of the Willys-Overland vehicle rose, classified officially as 'MA' and later 'MB', the name

Jeep became synonymous with it, and was soon a household word.

Many people say it comes from the slurring of the acronym GP, for General Purpose. However, according to Col A. W. Herrington the name was used in Oklahoma as early as 1934 to designate a truck equipped with special well-drilling equipment.

Another source of the name is a test driver for products of the Minneapolis-Moline Power Implement Co. Company officials claim Sergeant James T. O'Brien, while attached to the 109th Ordnance Co. at Fort Ripley in mid-1940, participated in a test of 'four- or six-wheel vehicles' designed by the firm. He reportedly called the vehicle a 'Jeep' after the character 'Eugene the Jeep' in the 1936 Popeye comic strip by E. C. Segar – a small, impish animal which could travel back and forth between dimensions and solve all sorts of problems.

The reference to Eugene the Jeep prompted an April 1944 editorial in the *Washington Post*. 'As to the origin of the monosyllable [Jeep], there appears to be neither

By the mid-1960s, the CJ-5 had become a much more civilised vehicle and remarkably similar to the current Wrangler. This is a 1966 model.

By 1971, it had become more of a recreational tool, with typically lairy 1970s paintwork, while that front adornment definitely wasn't from the official accessories catalogue! This is the Renegade II version.

mystery nor controversy. It first appeared as a generic name of an amiable and exotic creative of indeterminate sex, introduced about the middle of the 1930s into what was then a highly popular comic cartoon strip.'

Irving 'Red' Hausmann, a Willys-Overland test driver who drove the first pilot model to Camp Holabird, recalled: 'I took a lot of pride in the vehicle we developed, and I didn't like people confusing it with the Bantam Blitz Buggy or the Ford GP, so I picked up the name that the soldiers at Camp Holabird had been using.'

Red didn't invent the word Jeep, but he certainly gave it exposure. He gave a demonstration ride to a group of dignitaries in Washington, and among them was Katherine Hillyer, a *Washington Daily News* reporter. During the demo he referred to the vehicle as a 'Jeep' and Hillyer's article appeared in the newspaper on 20 February 1941, with a photo captioned 'Jeep Creeps Up Capitol Steps'.

The late General George C. Marshall called the Jeep: 'America's greatest contribution to modern warfare.' It served in every Second World War campaign as a litter-bearer, machine gun firing mount, reconnaissance

vehicle, pick-up truck, frontline limousine, ammunition bearer, wire-layer and taxi.

In the Ardennes during the 1944–45 Battle of the Bulge, Jeeps loaded with stretchers and draped with wounded, raced to safety ahead of spearheading Nazi armour. In the sands of the Sahara, the morass of New Guinea and the snow fields of Iceland, Jeeps hauled the .37mm anti-tank cannons to firing sites.

In Egypt, Britain used a combat patrol of Jeep vehicles to knock out a fleet of fuel tankers en route to Rommel's armour forces on the eve of the battle of El Alamein.

At Guadalcanal, Jeep vehicles went in with the US Marines.

Even before the war ended, Willys-Overland was planning to build Jeeps for agricultural purposes. This led to the first Jeep Universal in 1945, the CJ2A, featuring a tailgate and windscreen wipers. An all-steel station wagon followed in 1946. As more features and different models were introduced, the go-anywhere peace-time influence of Jeep spread around the world.

It's an open secret that the very first Land Rover prototype used many Jeep components in its quest to equal the GI's favourite steed for civilian work. Although many Jeep vehicles were in the UK when the

Right: One of the first and one of the latest − an illustration to emphasise the importance of evolution rather than revolution.

first Land Rover went on sale in 1949, it was to be many years before they were imported and offered for sale here again. Chrysler Jeep Imports UK was established in 1993, since when Jeep sales have snowballed.

In 1954, the CJ5 was introduced and became so popular that it endured, albeit with improvements, all the way to 1986, when it was replaced by the Wrangler. This introduced new levels of comfort and sophistication yet still embodied all the tough qualities that have made Jeep the world's favourite four-wheel-drive vehicle.

The Jeep name became so distinctive and distinguished that, on 13 June 1950, Willys-Overland registered it as an international trademark, which today is owned by the Chrysler Corporation after it acquired American Motors, the descendant of Willys-Overland, in 1987.

The final 'CJ' Jeep was the CJ-8, which gave way to the first of the Wranglers, the YJ in 1986. It continued the theme which was started in the 1970s, namely one of catering for the recreational market.

The YJ Jeep Wrangler

In January 1993, the YJ incarnation of the original Jeep – the Wrangler – became available for the first time in right-hand drive (RHD). Two engine options were announced, a four-cylinder, 2.5-litre and the much-used (and revered) 4-litre six-cylinder engine (which didn't actually become available until May 1993). The prices were £12,495, £14,395 and £14,995 starting with the base 2.5-litre car passing through the standard 4.0-litre and ending up at the 4.0L Limited (which had such luxuries as alloy wheels and leather seats. The Wrangler was built on a separate, lightweight, rectangular-shaped tubular frame chassis. Body panels were steel, with extensive use of galvanised steel for added protection of vulnerable areas of the body. All models were fitted with hard-tops which were removable to provide full open-air motoring. The folding soft-top was an optional extra, and all three models had power steering.

The 4WD system was Command-Trac, which put the drive to the rear wheels only for on-road use through a

conventional five-speed gearbox. Four-wheel drive could be selected on the move for off-roading or hazardous road conditions and a transfer box added a set of low-ratio gears for particularly hard going. The standard Trac-Loc differential allowed up to 60 per cent locking of the rear axle, which permitted forward progress even if one of the rear wheels had lost all contact with the ground.

One of the most important aspects for the style-conscious Wrangler buyers was the availability of a wide range of official Jeep accessories, which already included soft-tops, side bars, A frames, driving lights, bonnet decals and off-road tyres.

The new Jeep introduced in 1997 (the TJ) was a big improvement over its predecessor, due largely to the change from leaf springs to coil springs and dampers. This cutaway illustration was designed to emphasise this to an eager public. But despite this, for many Jeep enthusiasts the biggest improvement was ... the reversion to round headlamps instead of the previous rectangular versions! Things got so bad with the previous model, that many Americans had taken to wearing T-shirts emblazoned with the logo: 'Real Jeeps have round headlamps'.

On the inside, the TJ has become ever more luxurious, with padded dash, a stereo system, carpets and airbags all on the spec list.

The Jeep in its natural habitat, with a three-day weather forecast of 'scorchio'. It's hard to beat this kind of top down driving especially when there's the choice of on or off-road. However, the Wrangler can cope with just about anything ...

The big Wrangler news in March of 1994 was that both 4.0L models were available with automatic transmission. The unit chosen was Chrysler's well-proven three-speed automatic gearbox, fitted with a locking torque converter for increased fuel efficiency. Allied to the powerful and torquey six-cylinder motor, it was an excellent combination.

At the October 1994 British Motor Show, a number of improvements were announced for the '95 model year, the most practical being a revised ratio rack for greater steering precision. In addition, two new versions were introduced: the entry-level Wrangler 2.5 Sport and at the top of the tree, the Limited versions were replaced by the 4.0 Sahara. This model featured unique interior trim with special green and tan 'trailcloth' seats top stitched and piped in a contrasting colour. There were also useful pockets fitted to the rear of the front seats. You could also have the Sahara in any colour you liked – so long as it was Light Pearlstone (a suitably subtle sandy shade), or Moss Green metallic. To account for the improvements, the average price increase was around £400.

The prices of the Wrangler range at this time were:

Wrangler 2.5 Sport	£13,895
Wrangler 4.0 Sport	£15,495
Wrangler 4.0 Sahara	£15,995
Wrangler 4.0 Sport Auto	£16,395
Wrangler 4.0 Sahara Auto	£16,895

The TJ Jeep Wrangler 1997

In March 1997, Jeep decided to celebrate its fourth birthday over here, by launching a brand-new Wrangler model, the TJ. Not surprisingly, the design capitalised on many of the styling cues that made Jeep an icon over the 56 years since the launch of the original 1941 US military Willys MB. The aim was to keep the character of a traditional Jeep while improving it to provide customers with a vehicle that was more refined and capable both on and off-road. As assignments go, this was a tough one.

What followed was a subtle but near-complete redesign of the Wrangler exterior and a total reworking of the interior. 'The new Wrangler contrasts with all modern styling clichés,' said Trevor Creed, Design Director Jeep/Truck, Car Interior and Colour & Trim. 'It is a timeless yet contemporary design which keeps the legendary character of the vehicle.'

At first glance, the 1997 Wrangler was like looking at an old friend, the overall appearance being reassuringly familiar, but over three quarters of the parts were redesigned and every body panel, with the exception of the doors and tailgate, were changed.

Arguably one of the most important changes was the move to coil spring suspension, rather than the 'cart' springs which had dated the car so badly. The layout was similar to that on the Grand Cherokee, and mandated a front-end change, yet the signature Jeep grille and round headlights meant the traditional Jeep look was retained.

'The change to round headlamps not only recaptured the familiarity of older Jeep models, but gave us the opportunity to offer a better headlamp at a reduced cost,' said John Sgalia, Manager, Jeep Exterior Design Studio. 'On top of that, Wrangler owners – in true outspoken fashion – started wearing T-shirts that read: "Real Jeeps don't have square headlamps"!'

The improved suspension produced more wheel travel and so the front wheelarches had to be redesigned to provide more tyre clearance. Another comment from Sgalia: 'We knew that many of our customers liked to put larger tyres on their Wranglers, so the redesigned front fenders gave us the opportunity to offer larger tyres initially, thereby benefiting our customers.'

Exterior

Exterior form followed the functional need to package an integrated HVAC (heating, ventilation and air conditioning) system, and a passenger airbag. The cowl was raised about one inch to accommodate the HVAC unit which gave the hood a 'sloping' line in the side view which contributes to a more solid appearance.

The wiper motor was relocated from inside the cabin to the plenum and the flat folding windscreen was moved forward at the base for improved aerodynamics while maintaining its traditional fold-flat capability.

Another functional change requested by Wrangler owners was the relocation of the fuel filler cap. Previously positioned behind the numberplate carrier for the '97 models it was recessed in the side of the vehicle, behind the left rear tyre, increasing the ease of fuelling and eliminating fuel spit back. The numberplate was protected by a moulded bracket.

In keeping with the rough and tough outdoor image, wow hooks, hood latches, door and swing gate hinges were still exposed, but finished in matt black and more

... as this brave entry into the *Croisière Blanche* makes quite clear. The event is held annually high in the French Alps and is certainly not for the fainthearted.

flush with the surrounding sheet metal for a cleaner appearance and to meet world regulatory standards.

Wrangler Sports models had 15-inch wheels fitted with Goodyear Wrangler 215/75 R15 tyres. Sahara models had 16-inch five-spoke alloy wheels as standard, fitted with 225/75 R16 Goodyear Wrangler tyres.

Interior
The interior design was another area where the design team had to balance customer requirements and Jeep heritage. Although all-new, the instrument panel retained a rugged, functional character, but incorporated the modern safety convenience of front passenger and driver airbags. An extended centre

This Anniversary model Wrangler was produced to commemorate a staggering 60 years in production.

'stack' housed the radio, heating and ventilation controls, accessory switches and ash tray. Analogue gauges were grouped in a modern cluster unit with easy-to-read white on black graphics (inspired by the simplicity of Second World War vehicles and early Willys designs). A full complement of instruments was standard to support the Wrangler's functional character. The modular matrix of the interior could be rearranged to accommodate the requirements of both left-hand and right-hand drive markets.

'The interior of the new Wrangler is a much more modern design. It has been more carefully executed and is significantly more ergonomic,' said Creed. 'It was a major accomplishment for our designers to package so many components in a relatively small amount of space.'

The Wrangler also sported new consoles, moulded door trim panels that included map pockets with slots along the lower edges to ensure 'wash out' capability, and more supportive seat frames (derived from the Grand Cherokee) with new foam and trim styles. The new Wrangler also provided a rear seat that was 200mm wider than the previous models, achieved by redesigning the shape of the road wheel housing. In addition, the seat flipped forward to increase cargo capacity and load flexibility.

Both the soft and hard tops were completely redesigned for improved sealing, less wind noise and ease of operation. The all-new soft-top was supported by three hinged bows which folded rearward much like a conventional convertible while the new hard-top was substantially lighter than its predecessors.

Engines

Two engine options were available in the new Wrangler range, including the 117bhp 2.5-litre petrol engine, giving a top speed of 92mph a 0–60mph time of 13.6 seconds. The six cylinder, 174bhp 4.0-litre petrol engine was also available, with automatic transmission as an option. This gave the Wrangler a top speed of 112mph (109mph automatic) and a 0–60mph acceleration time of 8.8 seconds (9.5 seconds on the automatic).

The new Wrangler model line-up comprised four models, priced as follows:

Jeep Wrangler 2.5 Sport	£13,995
Jeep Wrangler 4.0 Sport	£15,495
Jeep Wrangler 4.0 Sahara	£17,650
Jeep Wrangler 4.0 Sahara auto	£18,250

(All prices are on-the-road and include Jeep's three-year/60,000-mile warranty and 12 months roadside assistance.)

In February 2001, the Wrangler range lost the smaller-engined mode and so the range comprised the 4.0-litre Sport, the 4.0-litre Sahara, and Sahara Auto. The Jeep Wrangler range was priced at £15,725, £18,350 and £18,995 respectively.

The following month, Jeep commemorated six remarkable decades of 4x4 heritage with a special limited edition Jeep Wrangler – just in time for the summer. The Wrangler 60th Anniversary model featured body-coloured wheelarch flares, 16-inch Icon alloy wheels, 225/16 all-terrain tyres, and 60th Anniversary badging combined with two distinctive exterior colour options – Silverstone and Black. Inside the Wrangler, the theme was continued with unique embroidered floor mats. The engine was the proven 4.0-litre unit.

The summer of 2002 saw the arrival of the Grizzly special edition. Based on the 4.0-litre Wrangler Sport, it came with 16-inch Icon alloys, spare tyre cover, 225/70 R16 all-terrain tyres and special 'paw-print' badging. Standard safety equipment included driver and front passenger airbags, height-adjustable front seat belts, high-level rear brake light, locking wheel nuts and a

It's tough enough for Lara Croft! Another special edition: just 75 TR2 Wranglers were made to mark its involvement in the film; *Lara Croft Tomb Raider: the Cradle of Life*.

Smart Key immobiliser. A tilt-adjustable steering column, tinted windows and a radio cassette player with CD compatibility were included in the standard equipment package. It was priced at £16,295 OTR.

The big news for cinema goers in 2003 was the release of the second *Tomb Raider* film, the *Cradle of Life*. It was double joy for Jeep fans because one of the vehicles at the disposal of the all-action Lara Croft was a Wrangler. To capitalise on the film's success, the Sport TR2 was launched, a limited special with a run of just 75 cars. It was based on the Wrangler 4.0 Sport and gained special Ecco wheels with 225 75/R15 tyres, a CD player with seven speakers and metallic paint (Intense Blue or Light Khaki). The price of exclusivity was £16,750 on the road. Simon Elliott, Managing Director of Chrysler and Jeep in the UK said: 'Wrangler perfectly sums up the Jeep brand – rugged, reliable, dependable, and the addition of the extra equipment

After more than 60 years, a direct descendant of the original wartime Jeep was displayed in military guise. The Wrangler TJL featured uprated suspension while the rear axle was 22in longer than the cooking TJ. (In the background is a hybrid-powered Dodge Ram.)

that makes the Sport TR2 will only add to its appeal.

'It's fitting that a car like Wrangler should feature in an adventure film and I'm delighted we are able to offer this model which links with *Tomb Raider*.

Military

What goes around, comes around; it's somehow rather fitting to finish the story to date with the 2004 military version of the Wrangler shown at the UK Defence Vehicle Dynamic Show (alongside a hybrid-powered version of the Dodge Ram). For the modern military, the Jeep Wrangler TJL had been modified to handle additional payloads with a heavy-duty axle, cargo bay and upgraded suspension. It featured seating for eight people and a wheelbase 22 inches longer than the standard civilian vehicle. Power came from a 4.0-litre PowerTech six-cylinder petrol engine mated to a five-speed manual transmission, or, for the first time in a Wrangler, with a four-cylinder 2.8-litre diesel engine due in 2005.

Cherokee pre-history

To a great many British readers, the Jeep Cherokee was introduced in 1993 – which it was, when the UK is taken *in solus*, but the Cherokee name had been attached to a passenger 4x4 many years beforehand. The name first appeared in 1974 on a version of the Jeep Wagoneer, which in turn had been around since 1962. It was an archetypal large, be-chromed American monster which gave little sign of the greatness to come, although the 1978 model featured creature comforts such as air conditioning, leather seats and a stereo, which certainly showed that the company was heading in the right direction.

Above: So familiar now, but quite radical back in 1984, this is the Cherokee Pioneer, a name revived in the UK recently for the panel van version of the Cherokee. Market research and input from (then) part-owners Renault, heavily influenced the final, car-like design.

Right: Hard to believe, but this is a direct forerunner of the Cherokee on your driveway.

Below right: This is the 1986 flat-bed truck version of the Cherokee, the Commanche, a pick-up based on an existing Cherokee model. Also seen here in this period press shot is Jose J. Dedeurwaerder, President and Chief Executive Officer of AMC.

Work on the 'new' Cherokee started in 1978 and its design and layout were heavily influenced by Renault, which had bought a large interest in the company (although overall ownership was still with AMC). The feeling was that, even though 4x4 and off-roading abilities were paramount, the vehicle should be smaller and more car-like, to appeal to drivers who would otherwise not consider an SUV (sport utility vehicle). In keeping with Jeep's traditional method of labelling cars, it had a two-letter code, this time 'XJ' for experimental Jeep. One interesting factor that came out of this European connection was that the new model was held together by all-metric-size fasteners – good news for current UK owners. When launched in 1984, the Cherokee was visually similar to the model which made its UK debut some nine years later, the most notable feature being its 'flattened' roofline. Chrysler acquired AMC in 1987, admitting openly that the 'jewel in the crown' was Jeep.

Chapter Two

Over here – the Cherokee

No matter how you look at it, American cars have never sold well in the UK. One reason is their love of the V8 engine which, as most are five litres capacity or more, is never going to be a plus point in Britain. Over there, with petrol cheaper than milk, an mpg figure which rarely makes it to double figures is acceptable. Over here, it decidedly isn't. The other major factor is also one of size; the vehicles tend to be on the larger side of

very big indeed. Again, no problem in a place like the USA where roads are wide and long, but in a country with 30 million cars fighting for space on overcrowded, under-funded roads, it is rather more of an issue.

Finally, we have the handling – or rather lack of it. Vehicles designed to drive for hours at a time on highways where a corner is a major event, are not best

Left: When you live way out in the American wilderness, miles from anywhere and just cart tracks for roads, you'll need a car. That'll be a Jeep then. (Nick Dimbleby)

Below: On this early model, 'square' is the order of the day, with sharp edges everywhere. The only visible extras here are the rock rails seen under the doors. All Cherokees rode on stylish alloy wheels. (Nick Dimbleby)

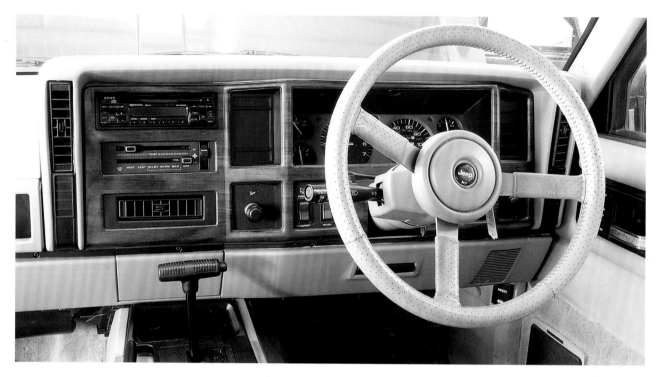

Like most American cars, the Cherokee came loaded with standard goodies usually found on the UK 'extras' list. However, the general dash layout was often – and quite reasonably – regarded as being like the inside of a Jukebox. The wood was actually plastic except on the SE models, which also received leather door and dashtop trim. The latter gave some problems when excess heat from the sun made the leather curl and pull the dash with it.

Multi-adjustable seats were very welcome in 1993, although again, the heavily chromed switches were very un-European.

suited to driving on this tiny island. Of course, the steering wheel is on the wrong side, but that would be fairly simple to sort, all things being equal. These factors have always been in place, but it could be argued still further that, of all possible launch dates, 1993 really wasn't the best time to launch a luxury, 4-litre off-roader in the UK. At that time, the country's economy was still in free-fall after the late 1980s excesses, with unemployment rampant, car crime rocketing and the buzz-phrase of the moment being 'negative equity'. It's a testament to the product that the Cherokee not only survived in this extremely inhospitable climate, but flourished.

Launch date – invasion UK

On 22 August 1991 a press release was issued announcing that American-built Chrysler and Jeep vehicles would be launched in the UK from 1992 following the appointment by the Chrysler Corporation TKM Automotive Ltd as its distributor in the United Kingdom and Ireland. Following the formation of Dover-based Chrysler Jeep Imports UK by TKM Automotive, the four-wheel-drive Jeep Cherokee was to lead the range into the UK market, thus becoming the first Chrysler model for right-hand drive production. Indeed, it was the first volume production vehicle to be built in RHD for export to the UK by any North American car manufacturer.

Chrysler Jeep Imports UK proposed to display the Cherokee publicly for the first time at the British

International Motor Show, Birmingham in October 1992. Although introduction dates were not final, models initially scheduled to join the Cherokee in the UK included the Jeep Wrangler and the V10-engined Viper R/T 10-cylinder high-performance sports car. The Jeep Cherokee had been selected as the first vehicle to be built for RHD markets as it was already Chrysler's major export model, being sold in 75 countries world-wide.

On 15 January 1993, factory-built right-hand-drive versions of the five-door Jeep Cherokee (and the Jeep Wrangler) spearheaded the Chrysler Corporation's return to the UK market. At this time, more than 1.25 million Cherokees had already been sold world-wide and over 5,000 serious enquiries were taken at the Birmingham motor show in 1992, and a substantial number of firm orders were taken by dealers long before vehicles arrived.

As we've come to expect from American vehicles, it came with a high specification as standard, surprisingly low prices and a comprehensive three-year, 60,000-mile warranty. If nothing else, all these factors combined to make the car-buying public sit up and take notice. Cheap 4x4s could always be bought, but there was always a trade-off; either the build-quality was awful and/or practically everything other than the steering wheel were 'optional extras'. Clearly, neither of those applied to this newcomer.

Richard Mackay, then Managing Director of Chrysler Jeep Imports UK, said: 'The return of the rejuvenated

Not much difference on this 1995 model year car, save for the rather neat pepper-pot wheels and a slight change to the design of the front wheelarch flares. (Nick Dimbleby)

Chrysler, through its world renowned Jeep products, is the most significant arrival on the four-wheel-drive market for many years.

Inside there was a different steering wheel with airbag, complex, turn indicator stalk and radio controls on the wheel. (Nick Dimbleby)

Left: The newly facelifted Cherokee raced into the picture during 1997. Outside there were lots of small changes, most aimed at rounding off those square edges. The front quarter lights disappeared, front and rear bumper mouldings flowed neatly into the wheelarch extensions and at the rear ... (Nick Dimbleby)

Above: ... a similar honing process had been applied to the edges of the tailgate (now steel instead of glassfibre) and to the lamp clusters. The rear screen was now bonded.

'Sales of 4x4 vehicles have been booming, even without the biggest name in four-wheel drive: Jeep. That sector is going to continue to increase and we are now contributing to that growth with our aggressively priced and superbly equipped Jeep Wrangler and Jeep Cherokee models.

'These will provide tough opposition for other 4x4 marques and we know from the staggering reaction we experienced at the motor show, and more recently to our new advertising campaign, that the British public just can't wait to get their hands on a new Jeep.

'There is no other 4x4 vehicle with the heritage to match that of Jeep – which began the whole four-wheel-drive movement back in 1941 with those famous

DID YOU KNOW?

In 1989, a two-door Cherokee model was introduced in the USA. Never available in the UK, it was aimed directly at the 'youth' market and featured the perennial six-cylinder, 4-litre engine coupled with a five-speed manual gearbox.

Although the specifications reached ever skyward, Jeep always took pains to emphasise that this was still a capable vehicle when the tarmac stopped.

general-purpose military vehicles. Jeep has had 50 glorious years around the world – now it's going to have a great future in the UK.' So, no lack of confidence there, then! A benefit of the Cherokee, and one which isn't immediately obvious, is that unlike some taller 4x4s, it can actually fit on *Le Shuttle* trains for travelling through the Channel Tunnel.

Launch line-up

In January 1993, the Cherokee line-up comprised two versions: the Cherokee 4.0 Limited, and Jeep's flagship, the Cherokee Limited SE (special equipment), with a third, the Cherokee 2.5 Sport, launched in May.

The Limited and SE models had the 4.0-litre six-cylinder engine, automatic transmission and a long list of luxury equipment. Prices began at £15,995 for the Cherokee 2.5 Sport and rose to £18,995 for the well-

equipped Cherokee 4.0 Limited, which was (rightly) expected to be Jeep's biggest UK seller. The Cherokee Limited SE cost £21,745. To add to the misery of rival manufacturers, all Cherokees were covered by the Jeep Privilege Service, which provided a three-year or 60,000-mile warranty, 12 months roadside assistance and competitive insurance rates.

The Cherokee Limited had a formidable list of standard equipment, including items which cost extra on many rival 4x4 vehicles (or in some cases weren't available at all). The specification included:

- Four-speed automatic transmission with power/economy settings
- Selectable 2WD/full-time 4WD/part-time 4WD Selec-Trac system
- Air conditioning
- Cruise control
- ABS brakes
- Alloy wheels
- Electrically operated windows
- Electrically operated and heated door mirrors
- Six-way electrically adjusted front seats
- Remote control central door locking
- Power steering
- Tilt adjustable steering wheel
- Stereo radio/cassette player with RDS, six speakers and electric aerial
- Integral adjustable roof rack

In fact, the only option was a leather interior! The Cherokee Limited SE had all of the above equipment plus leather upholstery and a special leather and wooden trim interior.

The Cherokee 2.5 Sport had a five-speed manual gearbox, power windows, power mirrors, power steering, remote control central locking, tilt-adjustable steering wheel, alloy wheels, rear wash/wipe, integral roof rack, a stereo radio/cassette player with four speakers and an electric aerial. All Jeep models had a single catalytic converter for reduced exhaust emissions and this of course, required unleaded petrol.

The Cherokee models, which had a light but ultra-strong uniframe construction for safety and durability, utilised two special Jeep selectable four-wheel-drive systems – Selec-Trac on the Limited and SE and Command-Trac on the Sport model. Both featured 'shift on the fly' capability, so the mode could be changed without stopping the vehicle. Selec-Trac gave the choice of two-wheel drive or full-time four-wheel drive for safer handling in wet or hazardous on-road conditions. For off-road driving, part-time four-wheel drive was available with high or low-range gear ratios. The Command-Trac system provided two-wheel drive for on-road use and both high and low-ratio four-wheel drive for off-road conditions.

While the clever 4WD systems had a long and proven history of effectiveness, the Cherokee scored many points by being very user-friendly on-road – which of course, is where the majority of UK 4WD vehicles spend most of their time. The Cherokee's handling and ride were better than most of the opposition and its wieldiness was aided by its compact body and small turning circle.

All models utilised a unique Quadra-link front suspension system, anti-roll bars and dual action gas-charged shock absorbers. Locating arms and coil springs provided maximum dynamic control. The ABS anti-lock braking system fitted as standard to the Cherokee Limited and SE prevented brake lock-up and provided improved stability and steering ability during heavy braking.

The multi-point sequential fuel-injected 4.0-litre engine of the Cherokee Limited and SE models produced 184bhp at 4,750rpm and 214lb ft of torque at

3,950rpm. These figures were impressive enough, but when combined with the car's light weight, they enabled it to outperform not just many rival 4x4 models but also many family saloons and estate cars; the official 0–60mph acceleration time was 9.5 seconds and the top speed was 112mph. The 2.5-litre Sport also utilised multi-point fuel injection and produced 122bhp at 5,300rpm and 148lb ft of torque at 3,200rpm. This model had a top speed of 103mph and a 0–60mph time of just 12.1 seconds, again, figures which many saloons of the day would have been pleased with.

In terms of carrying capacity, the rear load area could swallow 35.7cu ft of luggage (71.8cu ft with the rear seat folded), although not having a split fold rear seat was a bit of a bind. However, loading up was simple, thanks to the low rear sill.

Value for money

Jeep took great pains to point out just what value the Cherokee was, going as far as producing this chart, comparing it with the main rivals of the day, namely the Isuzu Trooper, Mitsubishi's Shogun and the (then) all-conquering Land Rover Discovery. An important aspect

Big, square vehicles like the Cherokee can be awkward to reverse and the Series 2 cars were often fitted with reversing sensors set into the bumper. This Meta Targa reversing aid is extremely easy to fit as an aftermarket product; two sensors are provided and they fit at either end of the numberplate, which in turn sits in a special bracket. No drilling required is a good thing when it's your pride and joy.

From 1997 it has been a legal requirement for all cars to have an immobiliser, but 'twas not always so and if your car hasn't got some security fitted, it is best to start now. A quality immobiliser – ideally Thatcham-approved – is a starting point, but add an alarm for extra protection. Good ones can be linked into just about anything else electronic (windows, sunroof, central locking etc.) to add day-to-day convenience into the package. For installation – go to a professional is the best advice.

to consider is one of quality; the usual argument against low pricing is that the vehicles just aren't built up to the same standard as the opposition. In this case, the Cherokee was easily as good as the rest and in many cases, better. Overall, the biggest Cherokee gripe had to be the out-dated rear leaf springs which weren't actually bad, but just not able to compete with more modern suspension.

Cherokee comparison chart as at March 1993

	Jeep Cherokee Limited	Isuzu Trooper Citation	Mitsubishi Shogun V6 Auto	Land Rover Discovery V8i
Base price	£18,995	£21,763	£21,512	£20,560
Diamond Pack (D Pack)	no	no	£2,634	no

Dimensions

Length (mm)	4,240	4,545	4,725	4,521
Width (mm)	1,790	1,765	1,785	1,793
Height (mm)	1,629	1,840	1,870	1,928
Cargo volume				
(seat up) cu ft	35	52	45	45
(seat down) cu ft	71	90	97	69
Kerb weight (kg)	1,489	1,900	1,910	1,986
Approach angle	43°	39°	41°	39°
Departure angle	32°	31°	27°	27°
Breakover angle	22°	20°	24°	n/a
Towing limit (kg)	tba	3,000	3,300	4,000
Suspension system	Coil/Leaf	Coil/Ind	Coil/Ind	Coil/Live

Engine/performance

Displacement (cc)	3,960	3,165	2,972	3,528
Max output (bhp DIN)	184	174	147	152
Max output revs (rpm)	4,750	5,200	5,000	4,750
Max torque (lb ft)	214	192	174	192
Max torque revs (rpm)	3,950	3,750	4,000	3,000
Max speed (mph)	112	106	100	97
0–60mph (seconds)	9.5	10.7	13.1	13.1
Catalyst	yes	yes	yes	yes
mpg @ 56mph	27.4	24.8	26.4	24.9
Fuel capacity (gallons)	16.7	18.7	20.2	18
Max range (miles)	457.6	463.8	533.3	448.2

Transmission

Permanent 4x4	yes	no	yes	yes
Select 4x4	yes	yes	yes	no
Auto hubs	n/a	yes	n/a	n/a
Man hubs	n/a	no	n/a	n/a
ABS	yes	yes	D Pack	no
Automatic	yes	no	yes	yes
Switchable auto	yes	no	no	no
Limited slip rear diff	yes	yes	no	no
Lockable rear diff	no	no	yes	no

Steering

Tilt adjustment	yes	yes	yes	no

Electrical features

Electric windows	yes	yes	yes	yes
Infrared central locking	yes	no	no	yes
Electric mirrors	yes	yes	yes	yes
Cruise control	yes	yes	yes	no
4 + speaker radio/cassette	no	yes	yes	no
4 + speaker RDS radio/cassette	yes	no	no	yes
Electric aerial	yes	yes	yes	no
Roof console	yes	no	no	yes
Air conditioning	yes	yes	no	+£1,404

Seats

Leather seats	+£1,000	no	D Pack	no
Electric adjustment	yes	no	no	no
Split rear seat	no	yes	no	yes
Rear head rests	yes	yes	yes	yes
Rear leg room (mm)	600	760	710	610

Exterior features

Alloy wheels	yes	yes	yes	yes
Wheel size	7JJx15	7JJx16	7JJx15	7Jx16
Tyre size	225/70	245/70	265/70	205R16
Black paint	yes	yes	yes	+£186
Metallic paint	yes	+£190	+£168	+£295
Mica paint	yes	+£190	+£168	+£295

Others

Warranty (months)	36	12/24	36	12

At the launch, Jeep had forecast an end-of-the-year sales figure of 2,000 units – combined Wrangler and Cherokee. However, just 99 days later the 79-strong dealer network had already sold 1,000 cars to eager buyers and the forecast had to be thrown out of the window. The majority of vehicles sold were, unsurprisingly, Cherokee 4.0-litre models and the company was on a high with the imminent (May) introduction of the Cherokee 2.5 Sport and Wrangler 4.0-litre versions.

By March 1994, the dealer network had been expanded to 82 and the company had registered its

5,000th sale. Moreover, it announced that while the first 1,000 sales had taken 99 days in 1994, the 1,000 sales figure took just 60 days. They were given even more to crow about when the April issue of the motor trade 'bible' *Glass's Guide to Car Values*, quoted a 1993 Jeep Cherokee 4.0 Limited with leather trim and a mileage of around 8,000, as having a second-hand value which was actually higher than its original showroom price!

'For the second-hand value of a vehicle to appreciate rather than depreciate is virtually unheard of nowadays, but this situation is a confirmation of the strength of the Jeep brand, its quality, reliability and its huge popularity in the UK,' said Richard Mackay, Managing Director of Chrysler Jeep Imports UK. 'It seems that the British motoring public simply can't get enough of the Jeep Cherokee.'

Indeed, it would seem so and he went on to point out that, 'According to this guide, a motorist could buy a Jeep Cherokee, use it for the best part of a year, sell it and make money into the bargain. How many other manufacturers could boast that?'

By the time the company attended the British Motor Show in October, it had even more good sales news – with more than three months of the year still remaining, Cherokee and Wrangler sales had already passed the total figure achieved in 1993. No wonder they were pleased with themselves! 'Four-wheel drive is still the fastest growing sector of the market and that growth has been fuelled by Jeep,' said Mackay. 'Jeep is continuing to establish itself as a serious player in the UK market.'

To get a real feel for the time, it is interesting to check out a few more detailed figures. During August, almost 1,150 Cherokees were sold, 20 per cent more than the combined sales of petrol-engined Ford Maverick, Mitsubishi Shogun, Isuzu Trooper, Nissan Patrol and Terrano, Vauxhall Monterey and Toyota 4-Runner models.

More facts to figure are that in the same month, the Cherokee (available only with petrol power let's not forget), almost matched the combined sales of the petrol-engined Land Rover Discovery and petrol five-

DID YOU KNOW?

In its second year in the UK, a one-year-old Cherokee 4.0 Limited was quoted in *Glass's Guide* as having a second-hand value more than that of a new car!

Another great safety and convenience extra is the SmarTire remote pressure sensing system. Small sensors are strapped to the inside of each wheel and these use radio signals to report both tyre pressure and temperature information to a main module in the car. This gives a readout of each tyre – even when the car is moving – and if the pressure drops below a certain point, an alarm sounds.

The tiny tyre pressure sensors are seriously robust and weigh only a few grams, so don't affect the wheel balance.

door Vauxhall Frontera. So far that year, Cherokee sales were 34 per cent ahead of the same period in 1993.

The list prices of Cherokees at this time were:

Cherokee 2.5 Sport	£16,695
Cherokee 2.5 Sport LE	£16,995
Cherokee 4.0 Limited (cloth)	£20,795
Cherokee 4.0 Limited (leather)	£21,895
Cherokee 4.0 Limited SE	£23,595

There was plenty going on in the 1995 model year, effectively from October 1994. All Cherokee models were blessed with a different steering wheel which featured a driver's airbag, while other changes included a redesigned steering column cowl and a new, less complex, turn indicator stalk. One of the reasons for its simplicity was that the cruise control switches had migrated to the steering wheel. The Panasonic stereo equipment featured removable front panels as a precaution against theft (previously the entire radio had to be removed). The seats were revised to offer more comfort and support thanks to longer squabs with more under-thigh support and wider back-rests. The head restraints front and rear were revised and the front seat belt stalks were now incorporated in the seat frames.

Early '95 saw the arrival of the VM diesel-powered Cherokee, very welcome in over-fuel-taxed Britain. The 2.5-litre engine took up plenty of space in the engine bay.

On the exterior, changes were restricted to the addition of a new colour – Moss Green metallic – and wider front wheelarch flares. The latter were slightly wider at the front than the rear to allow for the fact that the wings of the Cherokee angle in slightly towards the front. As such, the tyres had previously been slightly proud. Nothing is for nothing, the average price increase on the Cherokees being around £600, except for the Sport, which remained the same.

Diesel developments

Mooted at the Birmingham show of '94, but not actually available until the spring of 1995, was the long-awaited Cherokee diesel. This was particularly important for the UK market because of the swinging tax applied to fuel.

Research had shown what anyone could have guessed, that the 4x4 market was dominated by diesels, which accounted for almost 70 per cent of sales. As Jeep only had had petrol-engined vehicles on sale up until then, it was clear this was a gap that needed to be plugged.

The heart of the matter was a powerful yet economical 2.5-litre four-cylinder turbocharged, indirect injection diesel engine developed by VM Motori SpA, one of Europe's leading diesel development companies. The company, founded in 1947, was producing more than

All diesel models featured Command-Trac part-time 4WD and a five-speed manual gearbox.

60,000 engines annually from its manufacturing base in Cento, Italy. Highly respected for its marine engines – VM held a world speed record for diesel-powered boats – the company moved into the automotive field towards the end of the 1970s. Its latest automotive engine family, called Turbotronic, had been widely acknowledged for its reliability, durability and performance. (Among existing applications for the Turbotronic turbo diesel was the Voyager, Chrysler's popular people carrier which was then the world's best selling MPV with sales of 4.5 million already under its considerable belt.)

Turbotronic, mounted longitudinally in the Cherokee, had a cast iron block and a light alloy head. The design philosophy featured a tunnel crankcase, a single construction closed in a thin walled casting producing extremely high bending and torsional strength. Separate cylinder heads and circular crankshaft supports, both in aluminium, absorbed thermal distortion and mechanical vibration without negative effect. Purpose designed pre-combustion and combustion chambers, a redesigned turbocharger and the use of intercooling coupled with advanced electronics helped the efficiency of the engine, allowing it to produce almost 50bhp per litre.

The pre-combustion chamber was specifically redesigned to optimise the turbulence of the fuel-air mixture, breaking down the injected stream vortically in two directions. This improved combustion, resulting in an increase in specific power and a reduction in smoke and particulate emission.

Exhaust gas recirculation (EGR) helps to maintain nitrogen oxide levels within defined limits. A valve, modulated by an electronic control unit (ECU) intercepts and recycles the gas flow. The ECU controls the thermodynamic cycle of the engine, to avoid the release of polluting substances above fixed thresholds. Significantly, the engine's reduced emissions already met EC requirements for 1996 without a catalyst. Its power output was reasonable at 116bhp but as with any diesel, it's torque that counts, and with 207lb ft this was more than enough, especially as the peak figure was arrived at a lowly and very useful 2,000rpm. The engine took the Cherokee to 103mph top speed and the 0–60 sprint was accomplished in 13.1 seconds. The official fuel consumption came in at 39.8mpg, at a steady 56mph.

Jeep was keen to do a few comparisons with the opposition and they pointed out that the recently introduced Vauxhall Frontera could only manage 113bhp and 179lb ft of torque, despite the capacity

advantage of the 2.8-litre TD engine. It also produced more power and torque than the newly introduced Land Rover Discovery TDi and Range Rover 2.5DT. It was also able to out-perform some of the petrol-engined opposition, notably the Land Rover Discovery Mpi (max. speed 98mph, 0–60mph in 15.3 seconds) and Ford Maverick 2.4i (99mph; 0–60mph in 13.2 seconds). With its 17.6-gallon fuel tank, the 2.5 TD had a potential cruising range of more than 600 miles between refills.

The diesel model range

No fewer than five different diesel models were on offer, starting with the Sport and going up to luxury Limited SE specification. In between came the Sport LE and two Limited models, with either cloth or leather trim. Generous equipment levels had become Cherokee's trademark and the diesels were no different. All had electrically operated windows and door mirrors, infrared controlled remote central locking, power steering, alloy wheels, an integral roof rack and a radio/cassette deck with an anti-theft removable panel. As with the existing 2.5L petrol Sport model, all diesel models featured Command-Trac part-time 4WD with shift-on-the-fly 4WD selection. Like other Cherokee models, it continued to be built in the USA.

Jeep Cherokee 2.5 Turbo Diesel Sport and Sport LE

The range started with the two Sport models, which featured a driver's airbag, corrugated roll-formed steel side impact beams in the front and rear doors and head restraints in the front and the rear of the car. Black body mouldings with a discreet red insert provided protection against accidental parking dings. 'Pepper pot' alloy wheels with 225/75 R15 Goodyear Wrangler all-terrain tyres are also standard on the Sport.

A high-power Panasonic CQ-R30 stereo radio/cassette player with four speakers was fitted and the cargo area, which had its own illumination, had a retractable cover to keep luggage away from prying eyes. Two tie down hooks allowed bulky goods to be secured safely in the rear, and a fully adjustable roof rack was standard on all models. Both Sports had practical luggage cloth upholstery, while the SRS-equipped steering wheel was tilt adjustable. Sport LE versions added Limited-style upgraded door inners and wood effect was applied to door tops and fascia. Air conditioning, backed by upgrades to the alternator, battery, radiator and auxiliary fan, was available as an option.

Jeep Cherokee 2.5 Turbo Diesel Limited (cloth) and Limited (leather)

Limited models built on the already comprehensive Sport specification with extra luxury and safety touches. A three-channel, four-sensor, ABS anti-lock brake system was standard, along with cruise control and air conditioning. Front seats featured six-way power adjustment and an upgraded Panasonic CQ-RD40 RDS radio/cassette player provided the music. Other differentiating features included anti-skid strips on the cargo floor, body colour side-protection cladding, a roof console, leather trim for the SRS steering wheel and cross-spoke alloy wheels. Limited (leather) versions were finished with a ruched leather interior trim.

Jeep Cherokee 2.5 Turbo Diesel Limited SE

The ultimate Cherokee Turbo Diesel was the Limited SE, which enjoyed the luxury of Bridge of Weir leather upholstery with hand-stitched detailing to the fascia, glove box, oddment tray, cubby box lid, gear selector and the door tops. The opulent treatment continued with the addition of burr elm finishing to the instrument panel and gear selector surround, with leather and burr elm door inlays. The stereo upgrade was to the Panasonic CQ-45RDS radio/cassette deck with an option to plug in a CD autochanger.

Prices for the new Jeep Cherokee 2.5 Turbo Diesel at its March 1995 launch were:

Sport	£18,195
Sport LE	£18,495
Limited (Cloth)	£21,095
Limited (Leather)	£22,195
Limited SE	£23,895

Also in March 1995, Jeep took the opportunity to raise the prices of the petrol-engined Cherokees, thus:

2.5 Sport	£16,995
2.5 Sport LE	£17,295
4.0 Limited (Cloth)	£21,095
4.0 Limited (Leather)	£22,195
4.0 Limited SE	£23,895

A sporting addition

In November 1995, the low-priced Cherokee 4.0-litre Sport hit the streets. As standard, it came with automatic transmission, anti-lock brakes, power assisted steering, remote control central door locking, driver's side airbag and Selec-Trac transmission system. This was in addition to electrically operated windows all-round, electrically heated and adjustable door mirrors, a four-speaker Panasonic CQ-R30 stereo radio/cassette deck with removable fascia, tilt-adjustable steering wheel and dual illuminated vanity mirrors on the sun visors. The all-important price was just £18,995, which compared with £16,995 for the lowest priced petrol-engined Cherokee 2.5 Sport, and £24,295 for the luxurious Cherokee 4.0 Limited SE.

As with all 4.0-litre Cherokees for the 1996 model year, the engine in the new Sport version was modified to produce more torque at a substantially lower point in the rev range – now 221lb ft of torque at 3,000rpm.

Police six

May 1996 turned up an interesting Cherokee buyer – the Essex Constabulary! Half a dozen Jeep Cherokee 4.0 Limited 4x4s were acquired for use as traffic patrol vehicles in the county. This latest purchase meant that five police forces in the UK were now using the Cherokee for law enforcement (the others being Cumbria, Warwickshire, West Yorkshire and Wiltshire), although Essex was the first to buy a 'fleet'. At this point, petrol and turbo diesel versions of the Cherokee were involved in a wide range of active roles such as motorway patrol work, firearms support, rapid response, rural beat work and official senior personnel transport duties.

'We are delighted that the Essex police force has chosen the Cherokee. It is a vehicle which has already proved to be exceptionally versatile with police forces all over the world and now in the UK,' said Richard Mackay, Managing Director of Chrysler Jeep Imports UK.

'For example, one Cherokee 2.5 Turbo Diesel was used recently in a 48-hour period first as a rapid response 'blue light' unit on urban roads and country lanes and then the following evening, it was used to apprehend joy-riders who had taken to the fields in an effort to avoid arrest,' he added.

Economy records

In July 1996, Jeep was ever anxious to emphasise the importance of its new diesel Cherokee model and a record-breaking drive across Europe from Italy to the UK – on less than a single tank of fuel – seemed to do the trick. This especially, as there was still enough fuel in the tank on reaching the company's Dover HQ to drive the car to London and back.

More impressive still, it wasn't achieved at unrealistic speeds, as the 900-mile trip took less than 24 hours from start to finish and was completed at an average speed of just under 50mph. The turbo diesel Cherokee used just 15.4 gallons of fuel, equating to an average of 58.47mpg. The totally standard Cherokee was driven by husband and wife, John and Helen Taylor.

The fuel efficiency of the Cherokee Turbo Diesel even surprised the drivers. 'When we reached England, we looked at the fuel gauge and decided to carry on driving to the outskirts of London and then return to Dover. Even when we arrived back in Dover, there was still enough fuel in the tank, we believe, to have covered another hundred miles,' said John.

'When you consider that the vehicle was driven over some of Europe's tallest, fuel-sapping Alpine mountains, and through four hours of torrential rain in Switzerland and Germany, all at realistic speeds, the fuel efficiency of the Cherokee on this journey is truly remarkable,' he added.

The fuel tank was sealed in Italy by the official independent observer, PC Mark Kenwood of the West Midlands Police Force. He tracked the car across Europe and was present when the seal was broken at the end of the journey in Kent. The vehicle was a standard-specification Sport version of the Cherokee and no modifications were made to the car to improve its performance. The consumption figures were achieved using simple fuel-efficient driving techniques.

Auto Cherokees in particular can be very heavy on their brakes and when it's time to replace the discs, it is a good idea to uprate them. These Rossini discs, grooved and drilled for extra stopping power and better cooling are very efficient.

Facelift – 1997

The 1997 Jeep Cherokee cost $215 million – thankfully, this wasn't the retail price but the cost of the extensive, redevelopment programme, in other words, a facelift. The objectives behind this impressive cash outlay were:

- The adoption of an all-new interior, with improved passenger safety
- A stiffer body and chassis for greater refinement and handling
- Improvements to the heating, ventilation and electrical systems
- A package of noise, vibration and harshness (NVH) counter measures
- Improved quality
- Subtle alterations to the style and look of the car

The word 'subtle' is important here, because already, more than two million Cherokees had been built since 1984 (19,000 sold in the UK) and so there clearly wasn't too much wrong with the basic design! More importantly perhaps, was the fact, that in 1996 more Cherokees were sold in the UK than in Germany, France, Italy and Spain put together, so the UK market was extremely important and had to be kept on the boil. Let's look in detail at how those aims were achieved.

Body

From the outside, the most obvious changes to the new Cherokee were the subtle styling revisions. The popular and practical five-door layout was retained but the car had a slightly softer, more rounded look losing those sharp edges at the corners. At the front, the new seven-slot radiator grille echoed the design first seen on the Grand Cherokee, and was topped by more rounded front wings which now flowed smoothly into the 'A' pillars. Sculpted bumpers with rounded end caps reflected the softer style as did the new flared wheelarches, while a front valence/spoiler made for a neater, less angular, look at the front. At the rear, the tailgate was made from steel rather than glassfibre as previously and was more curved than before, while the

DID YOU KNOW?

When the Cherokee was 'facelifted' in 1997, as well as smoothing out the general shape, Jeep made the large rear tailgate out of steel; previously it had been glassfibre and therefore considerably lighter to raise!

hinges, exposed on the previous model, were hidden. A new bonded rear screen and one-piece surround blended into the design of the tailgate, while the look was completed by new rear light clusters.

The quarter lights in the front doors disappeared and were replaced by a one-piece glass window for better visibility and to reduce wind noise, while both sides of the car were protected against minor damage by deep side mouldings.

Improvements to the overall quality of the new Cherokee began at the very start of manufacture – in the body press shop at the manufacturing plant in Toledo, Ohio. All major body panels were now pressed off new or reconditioned stamping dies while 152 – some 50 per cent – of the body-in-white components were either new or heavily modified. Finer dimensional control was achieved through the use of geometrical dimensional tolerance (GD&T) principal location points on the body structure.

Interior

The biggest changes to the look and feel of the Cherokee, however, were found on the inside. Using themes from the luxurious Grand Cherokee, Chrysler aimed to create a more upmarket ambience without sacrificing the practicality so evident in the previous model.

Central to the interior was the new modular instrument panel, (then) the most advanced plastic instrument panel structure in the American motor industry. By combining many normally separate supports and brackets into one integrated vibration-welded polycarbonate and ABS plastic structure, not only was there a saving of no less than 4.5kg, but it also massively reduced the possibility of squeaks and rattles.

Use of the modular instrument panel also eased the production of left- and right-hand drive models on the same line – all Cherokees bound for the UK, Australasia and Japan were factory built in right-hand drive.

The new dashboard housed an SRS airbag for the passenger – standard on all Cherokees – and itself acted as a crash energy absorber. Instrument panels used simple white-on-black dials with orange needles for optimum clarity, while an overhead console provided storage space for sunglasses, as well as a trip computer and compass.

The computer's ambient temperature gauge was a rather impressive piece of design on its own, as it was made to ignore obviously false information; for example, when the car came to a halt, the underbonnet-mounted sensor would naturally record an increase in temperature, but the electronics would work out that this increase was due to heat from the engine and discount it.

Enhanced driver comfort was one benefit of a new tilt-adjustable steering column, while a vastly improved heating, ventilation and air conditioning (HVAC) system helped counter driver fatigue. Airflow had been increased by up to 30 per cent, the new cooling system and ducting offering improved performance with no increase in noise. The system had an eight-stage mode control which offered a wide variety of cabin climate conditions, while a single centrally mounted fascia duct gave quick, efficient defrosting. Rear seat passengers benefited from new ducting for both ventilation and heating.

A multiplex wiring system replaced the old wiring loom and gave the dual benefits of greater reliability and a significant reduction in weight. This 'intelligent' electronic sub-system was an industry first for Chrysler and used a new on-board data bus to exchange messages – both signals and data – to a number of key electronic modules, such as power train control, airbag module and so forth.

There were, of course, various special editions. This is the Orvis, one of many tie-ins with the big American fly-fishing specialist. It was available with either a petrol or diesel engine, with enhanced external features such as special alloy wheels ...

For the user, the benefits were improved reliability, because of the large reduction of components, and by using a common data link connector, service personnel could easily obtain reams of useful data, especially if a fault were present.

Other features included new seat fabrics, door trims, a revised steering wheel and a new floor console incorporating cup holders and storage compartments. The load area was fully carpeted and featured tie hooks and, on Limited models, a new load area cover. The standard integral roof rack system gave more luggage

... louvres cut into either side of the bonnet and a rear spoiler with integrated high-level brake lights. (Nick Dimbleby)

space on top of the car. A space-saver spare wheel was mounted within the load area under a protective cover.

Close attention was paid to reducing levels of noise, vibration and harshness and a comprehensive package of new damping and insulation materials was applied throughout the body. Tubular section sealing rubbers encircled each door to provide primary sealing against wind noise and water ingress, while revised door window rubbers ensured accurate glass location.

Chassis

The secret of the Cherokee's success lay in its combination of on-road comfort and off-road ability. Quadra-Link front suspension features a solid axle and coil springs while at the rear, the live axle retains the multi-leaf suspension. Clearly, a coil spring and damper set-up as seen previously on the Grand Cherokee would have been better, but with only a few years to go before a completely new Cherokee was to be introduced, it clearly wasn't financially feasible to carry this out.

As previously, low pressure gas-filled dampers and anti-roll bars front and rear (except the 2.5TD which had a front anti-roll bar only) helped provide the Cherokee with car-like luxury, while Jeep's renowned four-wheel-drive system ensured it would stop at almost nothing. Improvements were made to the rigidity of the galvanised, uniframe chassis and the body structure, the result being a 43 per cent improvement in torsional stiffness. This in turn gave greater strength, durability, better ride quality and more consistent handling precision.

Engines

All three engines offered in the 1997 Cherokee were familiar to Jeep owners, and incorporated the refinements already mentioned and introduced for 1996 model year improvements.

Drive train

The 4.0-litre petrol version featured the Selec-Trac four-wheel-drive system, linked to four-speed automatic transmission with a high/low-ratio transfer gearbox. Both the 2.5-litre petrol and 2.5-litre turbo diesel had a five-speed manual transmission with a high/low-ratio transfer gearbox coupled to the Command-Trac part-time four-wheel drive system. All Cherokee diesel models had limited slip rear differentials and 15-inch wheels – alloys on the Limited models.

Brakes and steering

The car featured ventilated discs at the front and drums at the rear, plus a new fourth-generation electronic anti-lock braking system as standard on Limited and 4.0 Sport models. The new ABS offered significantly less operating noise and greatly reduced pedal kick-back in use. Steering was as previously: the power-assisted recirculating ball type.

Warranty

Jeep continued its policy of providing an excellent warranty on its cars. All Cherokee models came with a three-year/60,000-mile mechanical warranty, six-year anti-corrosion warranty and 12 months roadside assistance, with extra-cost extension options for the purchaser.

The new Cherokee model line-up comprised seven models priced as follows:

Jeep Cherokee 2.5 Sport	£18,195
Jeep Cherokee 2.5 TD Sport	£19,495
Jeep Cherokee 4.0 Sport	£20,395
Jeep Cherokee 2.5 TD Limited	£22,895
Jeep Cherokee 2.5 TD Limited (leather)	£23,995

Inside was superb ruched Bridge of Weir leather upholstery, extensive burr walnut veneer trim (on dashboard, centre console and door caps), deep-pile carpets, and aluminium sill protectors. (Nick Dimbleby)

Jeep Cherokee 4.0 Limited	£22,895
Jeep Cherokee 4.0 Limited (leather)	£23,995

(Prices were on-the-road and included delivery charges, number plates, 12 months road fund duty and 12 months roadside assistance.)

In March 1999, Jeep launched a super-luxury Cherokee, the lavishly equipped Cherokee Orvis, in a second collaboration with the major American supplier of fly fishing and shooting equipment (reinforcing the 'outdoor' image of the car and following on from the success of the Grand Cherokee Orvis launched in November 1997). It was based on the top-selling Cherokee 4.0 Limited model, but with much enhanced specification. Either the 4.0-litre petrol engine or the more economical 2.5-litre turbo diesel unit could be specified, the price being £24,500 regardless.

Both models had special five-spoke alloy wheels, a rear spoiler with integrated high-level brake lights,

As the totally new Cherokee hove into view, the original Cherokee became the 'Classic'.

bonnet louvres and Orvis badging. Inside was ruched Bridge of Weir leather upholstery (seats, door trims and steering wheel), extensive burr walnut veneer trim (on dashboard, centre console and door caps), deep-pile carpets and aluminium sill protectors. Little Orvis touches included a specific spare wheel cover with extra pockets, a luggage compartment cover and an Orvis-badged leather document wallet and key fob holder. This was in addition to the usual mile-long list of goodies to be found on the Cherokee 4.0 Limited.

In October the Cherokee 4.0 truly became a 'Classic' – well, that's certainly what the badge on the side said, anyway. At £20,995, the well-equipped newcomer slotted into the range between the 2.5-litre petrol and turbo diesel models at one end and the Orvis flagship versions at the other. It used the 4.0L petrol engine allied to automatic transmission and Selec-Trac 4WD. As ever, there were plenty of goodies on offer, including

driver and passenger airbags, anti-lock brakes, air conditioning, alloy wheels, remote central locking, Smart key immobiliser, electrically operated windows and door mirrors, height-adjustable front seats, tilt-adjustable steering wheel, roof bars, tinted windows plus anti-theft radio cassette with four speakers and power aerial.

In September 2000, the Cherokee's time was almost run – at least in this incarnation. As such, Jeep took the unusual step of cutting the retail prices. The top-of-the-range 4.0 petrol and 2.5 TD Orvis models came down from £24,500 to £21,995 and the entry-level Cherokee 2.5, previously £17,995, dropped to just £15,995.

Overall, the 'square' Cherokee had been in production with very few changes for 16 years, quite astounding given that most modern cars are considered old hat after a couple of years. Its importance can't be over-emphasised, as it established Jeep as a world-player in a way no other model did and went on to become the best-selling Jeep model ever.

2001 – a Cherokee odyssey

In October 2001, the second-generation Cherokee was launched (the first new Jeep of the 21st century, and designated the KJ) which had a style that was far from

The new car managed to combine the luxury of the previous model, with the hunky chunky looks of the Wrangler, not least in the front grille design. Limited models had colour-coded bumpers and wheel-arches unlike … the Sport models, where grey/black plastic emphasised its sporting, off-road nature.

The all-new suspension, which ditched the rear leaf springs, meant that the new Cherokee was even more useful when the tarmac ran out.

its immediate ancestor, but in fact took a whole host of styling cues from those early, post-war Jeeps. This was most noticeable at the front, with the signature grille and round headlamps with 'eyebrows' extending into the huge bonnet. The muscular front bumper swept back into substantial boxed wheelarches, giving the Cherokee a powerful, rugged stance. The Jeep designers not only drew inspiration from the brand's past but also from the earlier Jeepster and Dakar concept vehicles. In America, the Cherokee changed its

name to Liberty with this model. The seven-slot grille featured prominently and the large grey plastic bumpers and wide wheelarch flares (as fitted to the Sport) helped give a more rugged off-road look. This built-to-last impression was helped by the fact that the wheelarch extensions weren't surface-mounted as previously, but set into channels in the wings.

All models received driver, passenger and side airbags, and an alarm/immobiliser.

The Limited models had colour-coded bumpers and arches. The doors were full-frame pressings and the unusual design saw them wrapping into the roof itself (shades of Lamborghini?!) and covering the windscreen 'A' pillars.

The new Cherokee followed the lead set by its Grand sibling (and indeed, most other modern large off-roaders) by dispensing with the old-fashioned separate chassis. A unitary structure sits atop chassis rails and for those who might consider this to be a retrograde step with regard to overall toughness, best think again; in terms of torsional stiffness, it was actually 43 per cent better than the Grand Cherokee! Anyone used to driving this sort of vehicle accompanied by a cacophony of squeaks, chatters,

A full-on side view shows how the trademark wheelarches had been retained while totally changing the overall look of the car. The neat rear lamp clusters echoed the round lamps at the front. Integral roof rails with easily removable cross bars were standard on all models.

rattles and groans will be pleasantly surprised with the Cherokee.

At the rear of the car, the huge, vertically opening tailgate was a thing of the past and was replaced by an upper window and a lower tailgate. The window is glass and opens vertically while the lower, steel, tailgate opens horizontally (unfortunately for RHD markets, it has to be accessed from the road side). The window can be opened independently by using the remote control fob or manually, by giving a gentle pull on the lower tailgate handle. If this handle is pulled out completely, the lower tailgate itself opens. Fitted to the top of the lower tailgate are a pair of rubber seals, one at each corner. Designed to prevent water ingress, they are apparently know in Jeep circles as the 'elephant's ears'!

With the doors opened, there's generous luggage space in the back and plenty of options, thanks to the asymmetric split-fold rear seats. It's a shame, though,

The interior of the redesigned Cherokee was not only one of the best Chrysler had ever produced, but arguably, one of the best around. Most owners opted for the rather nice leather trim and there were lots of neat touches with aluminium highlights here and there. The general layout and design were excellent.

In particular, the instrument console was both easy on the eye (and beautiful at night) as well as being logically laid-out. The steering wheel was chunky to hold and featured the cruise control switches.

that the rear seats don't fold totally flat; they rise slightly at the front. In the upright position, you can use the built-in hooks for hanging shopping bags, and on the offside and the lower tailgate, there is a handy luggage net for odds and ends. The 12v power socket is extremely useful, but it is unfortunate that a pull-over luggage cover is only standard on the Limited model. With security getting ever more of an issue, for those not so equipped, it is an essential tick on the options list.

The exterior design elements of the Jeep were carried over to the interior, including the door handles and door trims and circular air vents. Well-deserved plaudits were drawn for most aspects of the inside, not least the driver's view, which included stylish twin dials with satin chrome bezels for the Limited models. The Limited also came with upmarket options such as cruise control and a computer set into a roof panel. Of course, its beauty wasn't just skin-deep and the new car still retained Jeep's hallmark off-road capability.

The new Cherokee was wider and significantly taller, with a longer wheelbase than its predecessor but despite this, it also featured short front and rear overhangs – the holy grail for any serious off-roader – eight inches of suspension travel and two four-wheel

Above: The large, single-piece tailgate of the previous model gave way to a two-piece affair. The spare wheel had been moved from inside the car to an exterior bracket.

Right: The top section was glass and opened vertically, either on its own (via the handle or remote fob), or in conjunction with the horizontally opening lower tailgate.

drive options: Command-Trac and Selec-Trac. Mindful of those wanting to get physical with hostile terrain, all were fitted with a shield under the engine to prevent off-road damage, with transmission and fuel tank guards as options.

Each Jeep had to pass a series of durability trials derived from the tests that made the original Willys MB combat ready. So, while it is doubtful if any of us will ever need to drive our Jeeps into a combat zone, it is reassuring to know it has earned its stripes in the most stringent of engineering tests in the 4x4 world.

The engine line-up

The new Cherokee came with a choice of three new engines. First up (although not available in the UK until Spring 2002) was a 2.4-litre, DOHC, 16-valve four-cylinder petrol unit which had plenty of power, at

147bhp, and balancer shafts to make it smoother-running. Cars so-powered were mated to a five-speed manual transmission and Command-Trac 'part-time' 4x4 transfer case.

Next was the, 2.5-litre direct injection common rail turbo diesel (CRD) engine, featuring a cast-iron cylinder block and a one-piece aluminium cylinder head (in its previous incarnation, it had four separate heads), with 16 valves. This was descended from the VM diesel motor which powered the previous Cherokee. By the time of its launch, the VM company had been taken over by Detroit Diesel, itself owned by Chrysler. For UK buyers, who had to contend with ridiculous fuel taxes (and still do!), this was the most interesting, largely thanks to its fuel efficiency. At the top of the tree, the venerable straight-six, 4-litre engine was deposed by a more compact, 3.7-litre PowerTech V6 unit. Despite having a slightly smaller capacity, it produced more power and torque and came equipped with the five-speed electronic automatic transmission and 'full-time' Select-Trac 4x4 transfer case. The clever ABS system detected when off-road mode had been selected and recalibrated itself accordingly. There was plenty of performance from the 208bhp unit, enabling a 0–62mph (100km/h) time of 10.8 seconds and a top speed of 112mph. It returned 20.2mpg on the combined cycle.

Although it is tempting to believe that this is a relation of the engine fitted to the Chrysler Voyager, it is actually the Grand Cherokee's V8 unit with a couple of cylinders lopped off the end. Surprisingly, perhaps, it came with just two valves per cylinder, decidedly low-tech for a 21st century engine.

Happily, the new model featured independent front suspension, a tough and workmanlike double-wishbone set-up with the lower arm being forged iron and the upper arm, forged steel. The rack-and-pinion steering was a Jeep first and the camber and castor adjustment, while not unique, was certainly unusual.

Keeping everything out of the hedgerows was a revised braking set-up, with larger, more robust discs and drums with increased cooling capacity. More importantly perhaps was the integrated anti-lock brake system fitted to all models, along with electronic brake distribution (EBD). The latter automatically distributes braking forces between the front and rear axles and adapts to variations in road surface and load.

At its launch, the new Jeep Cherokee range started at £17,995 for the 2.4 Sport and rose to £23,145 for the 3.7 V6 Limited.

The 2.5-litre VM turbo diesel was available initially (and stayed in the catalogue) but the Mercedes-sourced 2.8 CRD unit was of far more interest to most. It was technically advanced, offering better economy with more power/torque.

The 3.7-litre, V6 engine replaced the straight-six engine which had done sterling service in the previous model. However, the new engine was lighter, produced more power and torque, and was more economical.

The 2.8 CRD arrives – over here and over there

The Christmas present for fans of diesel engines in December 2002 was the arrival of the larger capacity, 2.8 CRD engine in the Cherokee (although the 2.5 CRD remained and was sold alongside it). This unit, made by DaimlerChrysler, produced impressive economy – 27.4mpg on the combined cycle – while pulling the automatic car on to a top speed of 108mph and recording a 0–62mph time of 12.6 seconds. The prices started at £20,995. Importantly, it was the engine in the company's attempt to convince the USA of the value of derv-burners. Traditionally, America has always been one of the most diesel-sceptical countries in the world, but Dieter Zetsche (President and Chief Executive Officer of Chrysler Group) pointed out that the USA could reduce its oil use by approximately 800 million gallons and carbon dioxide emissions by eight million tons a year if Americans bought diesels at the same rate as Europeans. In Europe, 35 per cent of DaimlerChrysler vehicles were diesels while the 2.8 CRD-powered Cherokee/Liberty was the first diesel light-duty sport-utility vehicle to go on sale in America.

With the wheel out of the way, the asymmetric split-fold rear seats gave plenty of passenger/luggage options. It was a pity the seats wouldn't fold totally flat though.

Not all 'air conditioning' is actual air conditioning! This is aircon, where the driver turns a heat control knob as with a conventional heating system, but you can step up to climate control, where a temperature is selected on a digital readout and the electronics keep it at that level until you change it.

DID YOU KNOW?

Jeep often raids its heritage for modern vehicle names; the Cherokee Pioneer commercial of 2004 was named after a flat-bed version of the Cherokee launched in America in 1989. The Renegade name has appeared no fewer than three times; it was first used in 1970 for a special-edition CJ-5 model, then later in 1991–94, for a special edition Wrangler and then in 2005, for the top-of-the-range Cherokee in the facelifted line-up.

Extremely interesting

The summer of 2003 saw the introduction of another special edition Cherokee – the Extreme Sport. It came with unique 16-inch alloy wheels and extended wheelarches, bumpers and a front grille in high-gloss graphite. There was a choice of the 2.8 CRD or 3.7 V6 engine, both of which came with an automatic gearbox, five-speed and four-speed respectively. Standard safety and security equipment on both cars included driver and front passenger airbags, height-adjustable front seat belts, high-level rear brake light, locking fuel filler cap and a Thatcham Category 1 alarm/immobiliser. A leather steering wheel, trip computer, height-adjustable steering column, auxiliary power socket and six-speaker CD/radio/cassette were also included. Just 200 were produced with on-the-road (OTR) prices being £21,880 for the 2.8 CRD and £20,880 for the 3.7 V6.

Cherokee – Pioneer

Ever keen to explore new markets with slightly different variants, Jeep launched the commercial version of the Cherokee in March 2004. Named the Pioneer, it had more than 1,954 litres of load space and a payload of 359kg. The completely flat cargo area in the commercial version was created by replacing the rear seats with a full-length galvanised metal floor, finished with a hard-wearing minimum-slip carpet for load security. The rear quarter glass and rear door glass were removed and replaced with body-colour aluminium panels, although the doors were still fully operational, making access to loads at the front much easier. A removable floor-to-ceiling metal/mesh bulkhead was a £200 option. The Pioneer, based on the

Only 200 Extreme Sport models were made in 2003. They ran on unique alloy wheels and the extended wheelarches, bumpers and grille were finished in high-gloss graphite. There was a choice of power – either the 2.8 CRD or 3.7 V6 engine was available.

Above: The Pioneer was the commercial version of the Cherokee, with panels instead of rear windows in the doors – although the doors still operated. There was plenty of load space, but I don't think that horse will fit in there!

Left: Sound systems are important to modern-day Cherokee-ists. This is the cassette/radio/CD player as fitted to top-spec 2004 models.

2.5 CRD Sport model with 5-speed manual gearbox, it featured multi-stage front airbags, headlamp levelling, air conditioning, ABS, electric front windows and a single CD player as standard, although alloy wheels were a £320 option. The colours were limited to white, black or, for an extra £210, metallic silver. The basic OTR price was £20,531, although most commercial purchasers were able to claim back the VAT.

The 2005 model Cherokee

Early in 2005, the Cherokee received an interior and exterior 'facelift' together with some new and/or refined engine and gearbox arrangements. As with any facelift, it is the exterior that is first in the firing line. In this case, the exterior appearance was 'freshened' with a new design of front grille, fog lamps, fender flares, body side mouldings and new standard roof-rack rails and wheels. All had a wider appearance thanks to a redesigned front fascia and corner fenders which followed the sweeping line of the wheelarches and mounted the park/turn lamps in a higher location for better protection. There was also room to accommodate a fog lamp below each headlamp. In addition, all models had new, more protruding side sills and a crisper body-side moulding. Two new pearl-coat exterior colours, Dark Khaki and Deep Beryl Green, were available on all models.

The Sport model came with colour-coded front grille and a front bumper with 'twin-tube' appearance for a customised accessory look. The Limited had a more upmarket treatment with chrome grille, body-colour painted fascias and wheelarches, and five-spoke alloy wheels. Both the body-side moulding and the roof-rack rails were chrome finished.

The new image leader was the Renegade, a name from the past*, suitably chosen to give a more rugged look. It featured a new flatter bonnet and taller grille, plus off-road fog lamps, tail lamp guards, 'bolted-on' wheelarches and large six-spoke alloy wheels. The Renegade also featured standard tow hooks, three skid plates (under the transfer case, fuel tank and front suspension), and an optional overhead light bar. Also on the outside were roof-rack rails, side rock rails and a skid plate below the front bumper, all painted a bright silver.

Jeep Cherokee Sport models rolled on 16-inch diameter 'Full-face' five-spoke steel wheels or optional 16-inch 'Mechanica' painted alloys. The Renegade came with the new 16-inch 'Icon' painted five-spoke alloys while the Limited models received 16-inch 'Mechanica' five-spoke machine-face alloys.

* The Renegade name was first used on a special edition CJ-5 model in 1970, joining as a fully-fledged model in its own right four years later. The name was dropped in the mid-1980s, but from 1991 until 1994 there was a Wrangler Renegade model available.

Interior

Inside, the Cherokee and Cherokee Renegade had lighter coloured trim to highlight interior space, while the centre stack bezel and gear selector bezel were finished in Silver Mini Carbon (Renegade) and Satin Silver (Limited and Sport). Two new interior colours, Medium Slate and Khaki, were available for all models, while the Renegade and Limited could also be ordered in Khaki/Light Graystone leather or Slate Grey/Light Slate Grey leather.

More comfortable front seats were 5mm longer, the seat inserts 10mm wider for 'larger occupants' and the backrest was wider at shoulder height. Seat comfort and improved lumbar support were achieved by using dual-density foam.

Changes to the profile of the rear cushions and back rests reduced the rear seat fold angle, providing a flatter load floor for increased utility and improving cargo storage.

For the first time, a satnav CD/tuner was available in the Cherokee. The RB3 system featured a 4.9-inch screen including full-colour display, with turn-by-turn route guidance navigation and voice instruction, seven different user languages, automatic reroute calculation, and a memory to store 50 custom user destinations as standard.

Also available was the UConnect hands-free communication system as a Mopar aftermarket accessory. This used Bluetooth wireless technology to

Importantly, the cargo area was nice and flat with a full-length metal galvanised floor. It was based on the 2.5 CRD Sport model and came with a 5-speed gearbox.

The new top of the heap was the Renegade, a serious off-road image machine with a name harking back to the past. The most obvious difference was the flatter bonnet and taller grille which did away with the headlamp 'eyebrows'. The wheelarches were bolt-on and housed the 16-inch 'Icon' painted five-spoke alloys. The 2.8 CRD VGT engine was a gem and produced huge amounts of torque.

provide communication between the driver's mobile phone (where suitable) and the vehicle's on-board audio receiver. Incoming calls could be heard through the car speakers.

The new instrument cluster graphics were attractive white letters on a grey background, the Renegade and Limited models getting stylish chrome bezels.

The new heating/ventilation/air conditioning controls – part of the centre stack – retained three rotary dials, but had separate AC and heated rear window select buttons. The electric window switches were relocated forwards to a near-horizontal placement just behind the gear selector – greatly improving ergonomics and ease of operation.

Above: The interior had some very neat touches, not least the use of alloy highlights in the manner of Audi and Porsche.

New 2.8 CRD engine leads Powertrain range

Under the bonnet, the 2.8 CRD VGT (variable geometry turbo) engine had been tweaked to a best-in-class torque output of 295lb ft at 1,800rpm, giving a towing capacity up to 3,500kg and a potential driving range of around 450 miles per tankful. In replacing the existing

Right: As in the Series 1 car, a roof-mounted console contained the interior lights and a neat display panel. As well as the usual warnings, it including useful information such as outside temperature and mpg (or litres per 100km!).

The 2005 Limited model was pushed even further upmarket with lots of chrome (grille, roof-rack rails and body-side moulding) and colour-coded fascias and wheelarches. Five-spoke 16-inch 'Mechanica' alloy wheels were standard.

2.8 CRD, the 16-valve turbocharged unit delivered 9 per cent more power and 11 per cent more torque, while bringing many noise, vibration and harshness (NVH) improvements. A total of 41 measures were undertaken in three noise areas – source, structure and acoustics. As well as structural items, such as improved-isolation engine/transmission mounts and a stiffer cross-member supporting the drivetrain, a total of 25 acoustic components absorbed and subdued noise, including an acoustic engine cover, belly pan, bonnet liner and transmission tunnel liner outside the cabin, and new noise-absorbing carpets inside the cabin.

'Our new diesel engine provides the torque of a V8, the performance of a V6 and the fuel economy of a four-cylinder', said Craig Love, Vice President of the Rear-wheel Drive Product Team and Core Team Leader.

The new 2.8 CRD VGT engine was mated as standard to a new NSG370 six-speed manual gearbox. Made in Germany, with hard-finished gears for improved gear-change quality and better NVH, this unit had a lower first gear for quicker take-off from standstill and brisker initial acceleration, and a higher top (sixth) gear for reduced revs, lower noise and better fuel economy when cruising at speed.

Optional for this engine was the 545RFE five-speed automatic transmission, which was shared with the Jeep Grand Cherokee. Improvements included quieter operation when shifting between Park and Drive and the fitting of a turbine damper to enhance NVH performance.

Two petrol engines complete the range

The 3.7-litre PowerTech V6 featured numerous improvements to enhance fuel economy, improve NHV

The prodigious torque produced by the 3.7L petrol and, more usually, the 2.8 CRD diesel made the Cherokee an ideal workhorse (and as here, to tow a horsebox).

and reduce operating noise, especially at idle. The engine featured a new 'thick' wall composite intake manifold, an acoustic foam pad in the valley of the engine block's 'V', two fully isolated composite cylinder head covers, plus camshaft profile and valve-train modifications to provide quieter operation, and a smoother idle. The standard transmission for the 3.7L engine was the 42RLE four-speed automatic transmission, which now featured an automatic variable line pressure adjustment system to enhance fuel economy.

The 2.4-litre I-4 petrol engine came as standard with the new NSG370 six-speed manual gearbox. This unit was available in all three models, i.e. Renegade, Limited and Sport. (Renegade and Limited buyers could choose from all three engines whereas the Sport was only available with the 2.4-litre engine.) The fuel tank on all models was increased in size by around 5 per cent.

In terms of 4WD options, Command-Trac was standard on all three models when fitted with the six-speed manual transmission. Selec-Trac was standard on the 2.8 CRD VGT-engined cars plus five-speed automatic transmission, and optional on 3.7L models.

A limited-slip Trac-Lok rear differential was fitted to all models as standard. The suspension, drivetrain and steering were carried over from the previous model as was the powered rack-and-pinion steering. All Jeep Cherokee models came with 288mm (11.3in) ventilated front discs and 284mm (11.2in) solid rear discs, backed up by ABS and electronic brake force distribution (EBD).

Safety features

The 2004 raft of safety features was carried over, notably multi-stage driver and front passenger airbags were standard, with side curtain airbags optional on some models. Front seat belts had constant-force retractors, with a pre-tensioner on the driver's belt and the enhanced accident response system (EARS) shut off the fuel supply immediately after an accident and automatically unlocked doors and illuminated interior lights five seconds after deployment of any airbags. The new car had a four-star rating in Euro NCAP crash tests.

Ain't life grand – the Grand Cherokee

By 1994, the Grand Cherokee had received accolades from the press and public alike, being voted '4x4 of the Year' in Belgium, France, Spain and Sweden and 'Best Off-Road Import Vehicle' in Germany. It was in March that year, the UK had its first taste of the Cherokee's bigger brother, the aptly named Grand Cherokee. OK, it was only available to special order and with the steering wheel on the left, but the most compelling reason to consider a purchase nestled (or rather, lurked menacingly) under the bonnet – a 5.2-litre, 212bhp V8 engine. This eight-cylinder monster pulled the big off-roader to a maximum speed of 116mph and to 60mph

from rest in just 8.1 seconds. Incredibly, it gave an official economy figure of 25mpg at 56mph, something due in no small part to the efficient sequential fuel injection.

As we'd come to expect by then, the Grand was loaded with equipment, notably driver's side airbag, four-wheel anti-lock braking system, four-speed automatic transmission, power-assisted steering, cruise control, CFC-free automatic temperature control

Left: The Grand Cherokee is every bit as capable off-road as its junior sibling.

Below: Available throughout Europe in LHD form since 1993, the Grand Cherokee fetched up on our shores with the wheel on the right during 1996. It was well-equipped, well-built and easily able to go head-to-head with more established large 4x4 competition. (Nick Dimbleby)

Above: No, the photo hasn't been printed at an angle, this early Grand is actually at this angle. Despite its abilities on-road, it still makes an excellent tool for off-roading.

Left: However, despite its creditable mud-plugging performance and raft of standard extras, there was still no self-cleaning option! (Nick Dimbleby)

air conditioning, remote-control central locking, electrically operated windows and door mirrors, and alloy wheels. The Grand Cherokee's elegant and luxurious theme continued inside with leather seats, ash veneer trim and six-way power adjustable front seats, trip computer, and a high-specification, six-speaker Jeep Infinity Gold sound system. Despite the

Above right: With conventional dampers and springs all round, there was no shortage of travel when it came to the rough stuff. (Nick Dimbleby)

Right: Very, very tasty – the 1997 5.9L V8 XL model. It was only available in LHD and to special order, but that huge capacity, eight-cylinder engine makes up for a lot – top speed was 125mph. Note special Ultra Star silver 16-inch wheels, and bonnet louvres.

high specification, the new Grand Cherokee 5.2 V8 Limited cost a very competitive £27,995.

The RHD Grand Cherokee was introduced to the UK in February of 1996, selling alongside the already established, although more compact, Cherokee. Having been around in LHD markets for three years, we were actually getting a tried-and-tested product – well-tried, in fact, as more than half a million had already been sold. The RHD cars were manufactured by Steyr-Daimler-Puch Fahrzeugtechnik GmbH, or SFT, which also built all left-hand-drive Grand Cherokees destined for Europe, as well as right-hand drive cars for the Middle East, Japan, South Africa, Australia and New Zealand. The production plant in Graz, Austria opened just under two years previously to meet world-wide demand for the vehicle. Production capacity at Graz had been designed for a maximum of 47,000 Grand Cherokees a year.

A five-door, five-seater, the Grand was much bigger than the Jeep Cherokee, being 212mm longer, 136mm wider and 52mm taller. As well as providing more leg, head and knee room for occupants, the Grand Cherokee offered 10 per cent more load space than its smaller brother. The uniframe chassis design featured extensive use of galvanised steel. It was sold under the byline 'the luxury limousine', and its standard specification backed this up.

The imposing stance was underlined by the body-coloured bumpers, door mirrors and front grille. For 1996, the grille was enlarged and extended to bumper level to increase cooling efficiency and integral fog lamps were standard. Body-coloured side cladding helped protect the body against minor damage on and off-road. The practical high-lift tailgate gave easy access to the luggage compartment and like the Cherokee, it came with integral roof rails and easily removable cross bars. There was a range of stylish colours available, viz. Deep Blue Metallic, Black, Dark Iris Metallic, Light Iris Metallic, Forest Green Metallic and Dark Rosewood Metallic.

Driver and front seat passenger airbags were standard, together with side-impact protection guards.

The 4.0-litre straight-six petrol engine was fundamentally the same unit as used in the Cherokee

4.0 Limited, but with a number of major changes for the 1996 model year. Developing 174bhp and an impressive 222lb ft of torque, the familiar cast-iron 3,960cc unit – which featured sequential multi-point fuel injection – was given a stiffer cylinder block, and a revised camshaft profile. In addition, aluminium pistons were fitted. In keeping with the car's luxury image, the engine featured a new insulated valve cover (steel rather than alloy) and a new main bearing brace to make the engine both quieter and more responsive. A multiplex electrical system was adopted for the 1996 models, which reduced wiring loom complexity and weight while improving reliability and serviceability. The quoted top speed was 112mph with a 0–60mph time of slightly less than ten seconds. Fuel consumption on the extra urban cycle was 23mpg.

A four-speed automatic transmission was standard, which as usual, featured high and low ratios. The Quadra-Trac permanent four-wheel-drive system was used, albeit with a few modifications over its original incarnation (1993–96), in particular the adoption of a centre viscous coupling, which allowed torque to be transmitted between the front and rear axles in any ratio from zero to 100 per cent. (Previously, it was a 50/50 split.) This added flexibility increased on-road driveability, reduced wear on components and enhanced traction off-road.

Disc brakes were fitted all round, ventilated at the front, and an ABS anti-lock braking system was standard. The power steering was speed proportional – when manoeuvring or parking, assistance was greatest and this gradually decreased as the speed rose. Smart 16 x 7J alloy wheels were shod with 225/70R dual-purpose road tyres (previously, 15-inch wheels and tyres were used). To match on-road comfort with off-road ability it featured coil springs all round with heavy duty gas-filled dampers and anti-roll bars front and rear.

Interior and equipment

The Grand set out to match the best offered by luxury cars and at the same time, set new standards for the 4x4 sector. An all-new fascia design (over the 1992

original) included a new instrument panel and more ergonomic positioning of major and minor controls. Leather upholstered seats were fitted, with the front seats being heated and featuring eight-way power control and powered lumbar support. The driver's seat also had a two-position memory. Dual airbags were standard while the rear upper seat belt mounts were height adjustable.

Other standard equipment included electrically operated windows, cruise control, tilt-adjustable leather-trimmed steering wheel and electrically adjustable, heated door mirrors. Automatic temperature-controlled air conditioning was standard, as were smart alloy wheels, central locking, wood-grain door and fascia inserts, roof console (with trip computer and compass) and a six-speaker high-quality stereo system.

In the rear, the load area was fully carpeted and featured tie-down hooks and skid strips as well as a retractable load area cover, load restraining net and quarter panel storage area. The rear seat was foldable, 60/40, for combining luggage and passengers. The full-size spare wheel was mounted inside the load area and had its own protective cover.

The only optional extras were a sunroof at £645 and a CD autochanger for £492. Importantly, all Grand Cherokees were fitted with an alarm/immobiliser, to Thatcham Category 1 specification.

The LHD Grand Cherokee 5.2 Limited remained available to special order at a price of £29,995 – although the power was now being quoted at 209bhp.

Again, Jeep made a price point by issuing a table comparing its pricing structure with the direct competition. For once, it is good to be at the bottom of the heap!

Mercedes-Benz G-Wagen G300	£42,500
Toyota Landcruiser 4.5 VX	£38,689
Range Rover 4.0 V8i SE	£37,200
Mitsubishi Shogun 3.5 V6	£36,789
Range Rover 4.0 V8i	£32,850
Range Rover 2.5Tdi Classic	£29,475
Jeep Grand Cherokee 4.0 Limited	£28,995

The diesel engine arrives

The big news in January 1997 was the arrival of a special edition Grand Cherokee – the Laredo – which was available with the existing 4.0-litre and, perhaps more importantly, a diesel power plant, the 2.5 TD unit as already fitted to the Cherokee. Mechanically the Laredo and Limited models were virtually identical, differences being restricted to tyre size (the Laredo was fitted with 15-inch wheels/tyres and the Limited with 16-inch wheels and tyres), and the engine and transmission. Unusually for a special edition, the Laredo cost less than the existing machines and both petrol and diesel cars were the same, priced at a very competitive £26,495 OTR.

The 4.0-litre petrol car was virtually the same as the Limited model, so we'll cover the TD version in detail. The 2.5-litre turbo diesel came with a five-speed manual transmission (no auto option yet) and a dual high/low-ratio transfer gearbox using Jeep's Command-Trac part-time four-wheel-drive system. Both Laredo models had a limited slip rear differential and 15-inch alloy wheels shod with chunky Goodyear Wrangler 215/75 all-terrain tyres.

The 2.5 turbo diesel was essentially the same Turbotronic unit supplied by VM Motori SpA for the Cherokee, which managed to meet EC emissions requirements without the need for a catalyst. It had a cast-iron block and separate light alloy cylinder heads. It also featured a tunnel crankcase, a single construction closed in a thin-walled casting producing extremely high bending and torsional strength.

Circular aluminium crankshaft supports absorbed thermal distortion and mechanical vibration without negative effect. Purpose-designed pre-combustion and combustion chambers, a redesigned turbocharger and the use of intercooling coupled with advanced electronics helped the efficiency of the engine, allowing it to produce almost 50bhp per litre.

Under the bonnet, the VM 2.5L diesel engine took up plenty of space. (Nick Dimbleby)

The '97 Limited Edition diesel version had even more toys than usual, although the driver still had to stir his own gears.

Exhaust gas recirculation (EGR) helped to maintain nitrogen oxide levels within defined limits. A valve, modulated by an electronic control unit (ECU) intercepted and recycled the gas flow. The ECU controlled the thermodynamic cycle of the engine, to avoid the release of polluting substances above fixed thresholds.

The engine developed 114bhp at 3,900rpm and 205lb ft of torque at a very low 1,800rpm. In terms of performance, Jeep claimed a top speed of 97mpg and a 0–60mph time of 15.9 seconds. However, economy is the watchword when buying a diesel and the unit produced over 30mpg on the combined cycle tests and an impressive 36mpg on the extra urban cycle.

Standard equipment on the Laredo models was predictably lavish although slightly less so than the Limited model. (It should be noted that all '97 model year Grands received a third, high-level rear brake lamp in accordance with UK legislation.) The most obvious ways the company achieved the lower price was by fitting cloth seat facings rather than leather (velour was an option), and by fitting air conditioning rather than full, temperature controlled, climate control. Nevertheless, there was still plenty to go at, as this list shows:

Safety and security
Driver and passenger airbags
Anti-lock brakes
Side-impact protection guards
Remote-control alarm and rolling code immobiliser
High-level rear brake light

Comfort
Air conditioning
Electric windows front and rear with one touch down for driver's window
Electrically operated, heated door mirrors
Remote-control central door locking
Tilt-adjustable leather-trimmed steering wheel
Cruise control
Cloth faced seats (optional velour)
Wood-grain fascia inserts
Cup holders front and rear

Exterior

15 x 7J alloy wheels
Integral roof rails
Chrome front grille
Dark grey bumpers, protective side cladding and exterior mirrors

Luggage area

Tie hooks in cargo area, plus retractable cover and load restraining net
Interior-mounted full-size spare wheel
60/40 split folding and removable seat cushions

In-car entertainment

Anti-theft radio/cassette with CD compatibility, six speakers and power antenna

Bigger – and better?

In total contrast to the parsimonious diesel engined-Grands, September saw Jeep announcing a very special version, powered by a monstrous, 5.9-litre V8 petrol engine! Launched at the Frankfurt Motor Show, the Jeep Grand Cherokee Limited LX became the fastest Jeep imported into the UK with a 0–60mph time of just 7.5 seconds and an electronically limited top speed of 125mph.

A number of distinctive exterior features announced to the world that this was no ordinary Jeep, including a front grille with mesh insert, large chrome exhaust tip, body-coloured sill mouldings and chrome badging. Also unique to the new vehicle were 16 x 7 Ultra Star silver aluminium wheels and P225/70R16 Wrangler HP tyres.

Inside, the luxury of the Grand Cherokee was reinforced with leather-covered door bolsters and arm rests, along with leather-trimmed centre console armrest, transmission, transfer case and parking brake levers. Bird's eye maple simulated wood-grain accents were used throughout the vehicle. The heated, 10-way adjustable power front seats were fully leather covered with premium calf's nap grain seat inserts.

The model also featured a new 180-watt sound system with 10 speakers in different locations around the vehicle including four housed in a soundbar in the rear headliner.

A new electronically controlled four-speed overdrive automatic transmission was fitted, which was optimised to handle the staggering 348lb ft of torque from the 5.9-litre engine, along with an upgraded, high strength output shaft on the NV249 transfer case.

The Grand Cherokee 5.9 Limited LX was only available in the UK to special order and, sadly, in left-hand-drive format. Three colours were on offer: Bright Platinum, Forest Green and a new body colour of Deep Slate. It was built in Graz, Austria, where around 35,000 Grand Cherokees were produced each year for more than 100 markets around the world.

The shirt on your back

It used to be that car manufacturers sold cars from their showrooms and the odd accessory or two, but the market for selling anything to do with a specific brand spiralled incredibly as the century drew to a close. As such, Jeep chose the October '97 British Motor Show to announce a collection of Jeep-branded clothing and footwear. This 'reflects the heritage of the name Jeep, with comfort and easy care requirements for every garment'. Available from November of that year in River Island stores in 50 UK towns and cities with the intention of expanding gradually into other retail and mail order outlets.

No limited luxury for diesel

By December of '97, the Grand Cherokee was the best-selling Jeep in the range and to capitalise even further on its success, the range was expanded to five versions with the introduction of a luxury version of the 2.5 Turbo Diesel model – the Limited.

It had the same high equipment level as the 4.0 Limited and the same price of £29,995.

'There has been a gap in our Grand Cherokee range for those customers wishing to combine the luxury and refinement of the Limited specification with the fuel economy benefits provided by our turbo diesel engine. So we are delighted to introduce this vehicle to meet that demand,' said Richard Mackay, Managing Director of Chrysler Jeep Imports UK.

The equipment included climate-controlled air conditioning, cruise control, leather seats, electrically heated power door mirrors, 16 x 7J alloy wheels, power-adjustable, heated front seats with memory setting on the driver's side, electric windows all-round, leather steering wheel, six-speaker radio cassette with CD compatibility and interior roof console with compass, outside temperature gauge, and a trip computer.

Five exterior colours were available, with no extra cost for special paint, and there was a choice of two leather trim colours. The only optional extra available was a sunroof, at £645.

The four-wheel-drive system fitted to the new vehicle featured 'Quadra-Trac' permanent four-wheel drive –

the first time this system had been available with the diesel engine – along with a viscous coupling and limited slip rear differential. The transmission, however, was a slightly less luxurious five-speed manual.

Fly fishing ...

In Britain, fly fishing immediately brings to mind J. R. Hartley, but in America, the biggest name in that particular sport is Orvis. In February 1998, Jeep did a little more lateral marketing when it developed a tie-in with Orvis, the result being a special edition Jeep Grand Cherokee 4.0 Limited called, not altogether unexpectedly, the Orvis. As well as the usual niceties from the 4.0-litre Limited, it had a long list of additional equipment including luxury agate leather seats, burr walnut wood veneer trimming, an electrically operated tilt and slide sunroof and a 100-watt in-car entertainment system with 10 speakers and CD autochanger. It was immediately recognisable from the outside by its unique 16-inch Ultra Star alloy wheels, a mesh front grille, bonnet louvres, extended sills, stainless-steel kick plates and new-style roof rails. The choice of colours was Forest Green, Bright

Platinum Pearl Coat and Deep Slate Pearl Coat – the last two being unique to the Orvis.

'Both the Jeep and Orvis brands appeal to similar customer groups. They are American, rugged and the best in their respective fields,' said Steve Gray, Marketing Director of Chrysler Jeep Imports UK. 'We are delighted therefore to be associated with Orvis in introducing this important addition to our range.' The new special edition had an OTR price of £33,495 and received a boost in April 1998 when Tamara Beckwith joined 'the Jeep set', making the Orvis her chosen means of transportation.

2.5 Turbo Diesel Limited

At the same time, the company chose to push the diesel-engined car ever further upmarket and this new model had the same specification as the award-winning Grand Cherokee 4.0 Limited. It was priced at

Early 1998 saw another special edition, the Orvis, which tied in to the American fly-fishing giants. The long specification included extra luxury interior features and unique 16-inch Ultra Star alloy wheels, bonnet louvres and two unique colours.

£29,995. Both models had a new system to enhance steering response and feel and for the first time, the diesel car was fitted with the Quadra-Trac permanent four-wheel-drive system as fitted to petrol versions.

Smooth operator

As the spring of 1999 got into its stride, it was boosted by the arrival of the revised Grand Cherokee. It had plenty to live up to, the outgoing model winning plenty of 4x4 awards and selling well; of the 80,000 that had been sold in Europe since its introduction in 1993, over 14,000 – that's 17 per cent – had been purchased in the UK (and remember, it was only available in RHD form from 1996).

February 1999 saw the facelifted Grand Cherokee arrive, with a much more rounded, complete appearance. This view shows a direct comparison, with the new vehicle at front sharing only 127 components with its immediate predecessor. Not quite sure about Metallic Purple, though!

The all-new Jeep Grand Cherokee arrived in the UK succeeding a model which had achieved a remarkable reputation around the world. Of course, the new model had a two-letter 'J' designation, this time it was WJ. Production of the new car began for the Americans at the new Jefferson North Plant in Detroit during the summer of 1998. In addition, production also started at four other locations around the world: Graz, Austria – from where all vehicles sold in Europe were sourced – plus Thailand, Argentina and Venezuela.

Volume production of the European version began early in 1999 in both left- and right-hand drive

configurations for the pan-European introduction in early spring.

The aim was, not unnaturally, to pick up where the previous model left off. It had to retain the classic Jeep design and impressive 4WD system while upping the ante in technical areas, engines, features and equipment.

Although initially looking very similar to its predecessor, the overall design was more fluid and refined while still retaining that latent aggression that gives any car of this type an instant appeal. In fact, there were only 127 carry-over parts from the previous model. At the front was, of course, the signature Jeep grille with its seven slots, sitting back at a sharper angle than before, as did the windscreen. On either side were jewel-like round quad headlamps and the stretched trapezoidal wheelarches made it instantly recognisable from the side. At the rear, the main distinguishing feature was the fitment of bold tri-colour tail lamps.

Although the new Grand Cherokee rode on the same wheelbase as before, it was 110mm longer, 54mm higher, 39mm wider and had a 38mm wider track. Step-in height was reduced by 28mm for easy entry, although the seating position was 25mm higher for an enhanced 'command-of-the-road feel'.

Interior

Inside, the aim was to offer luxury levels of fit, finish and refinement. The ergonomic design and significantly increased soft-touch surfaces created a solid, understated, yet elegant combination, while the blend of materials and textures added attention to detail. All the primary driver controls were placed at fingertip distance, grouped on stalks around the steering wheel, and most stereo controls were integrated into the steering wheel.

Occupants benefited from 20mm increased headroom at the front and 12mm at the rear and 78mm more rear hip space. Useable cargo volume was increased by 36 litres and although the full-size spare tyre was still located in the car, it had been hidden under the boot floor. As a result, the split-fold rear seats, with fold-down headrests, opened up a truly cavernous luggage compartment.

Under the bonnet

It was designed to take three engine options – two of which were all-new, but the diesel power plant didn't arrive until November 1999. The highly acclaimed 4.0-litre unit was carried over from the previous Grand

The interior specification never dropped below luxurious and more often than not, went well above it. (Nick Dimbleby)

Cherokee, but with significant improvements. For the petrol-head, it was the 4.7-litre V8 PowerTech engine, which created most interest. 'We chose to design these new engines with optimum displacements that would maximise fuel efficiency and minimise emissions, while setting a new level for performance and refinement,' said David Van Raaphorst, Executive Engineer – Powertrain. 'For the V8, it meant a smaller displacement – but more useable power, lower noise, vibration and harshness and greater durability than the 5.2-litre engine it replaces.

The spare wheel was housed out of the way under a false floor. This area is ideal for storing the net when not in use and is a favourite place for fuel converters to put an LPG tank.

The rear was more rounded and featured the chunky revised lamp clusters. Unlike its smaller sibling, the rear tailgate was horizontally split and the loading level was usefully low, especially as … (Nick Dimbleby)

… there was plenty of room for large loads of luggage. This could be extended as required by folding some or all of the split-fold rear seat. Four hooks in the floor for securing the cargo net are supplied.

'Engine efficiencies were key goals in the development process,' added Van Raaphorst. 'With the extensive use of alternative materials, plus our ability to optimise the air flow by using computer simulations, we have engines that produce more power, use less fuel and burn cleaner than the engines they replace. By increasing engine and overall powertrain stiffness, improving the balance of rotating components and upgrading the powertrain mounting system, we have made this V8 engine among the most quiet, refined and best sounding petrol powerplants Chrysler has ever developed.'

All three new engines were designed for:

Better performance – a new air induction system contributed to increased engine power by significantly reducing air flow restriction. Larger ducts and engine-mounted resonators were tuned to minimise flow restriction and induction noise.

Better fuel consumption – all models benefited from reduced tyre rolling resistance, a hybrid cooling fan system that reduced drag on the engine, low-drag brake systems and reduced aerodynamic drag relative to previous models. In addition, petrol engines benefited from lower idle speeds than those used previously.

Better quality and reliability – automatic tensioning made the belt system maintenance-free for 100,000 miles in normal service.

This also reduced peak belt tension, contributing to belt life and reducing bearing loads. A new baffle on the radiator closure panel protected against water and snow intrusion.

Lower NVH – noise levels were reduced thanks to an all-new body structure, quieter engines, new powertrain mounts, enhanced suspension isolation and an extensive list of silencing treatments.

The 4.0-litre, OHV, SMPI I-6

Upgrades to the 4.0-litre I-6 engine made it quieter, more powerful, cleaner and more durable in most areas. The new model had increased vehicle weight and larger tyres, however, these were offset by an additional 13hp which enabled the same level of performance to be retained. A new splitter-vane water pump was 50 per cent more efficient than its predecessor and on its own, contributed 2hp of the additional engine output. A new cylinder head with reduced-area exhaust ports and new exhaust manifolds more efficiently expelled spent combustion products, thereby also increasing power. The overall performance remained impressive, with a top speed of 117mph and a 0–60mph time of less than 10 seconds.

Despite this, fuel economy levels were improved by 12 per cent, thanks to reduced tyre rolling resistance, improved aerodynamic drag and lower idle speeds than the previous engine. On the extra urban cycle, the 4.0-litre engine was capable of a very healthy 23.9mpg.

To minimise interior noise and vibration stemming from the 4.0-litre powerplant assembly (engine, transmission, and transfer case), a set of steel struts interconnected these components. NVH refinement in the engine assembly reduced radiated noise perceived by the driver by a very significant 5 dB.

The 4.7-litre SOHC, SMPI V8

The previous 5.2-litre engine was a delight, but rather thirsty and so it was replaced by a 4.7-litre version. However, despite a decrease in cubic capacity – approximately ten per cent – it offered more useable power, torque and greater durability than the outgoing engine. The resultant driveability (how smoothly the engine responds under all driving conditions) was rated as the most important performance parameter for most customers. In conjunction with the new 45 RFE transmission, it also provided a stronger initial surge, faster acceleration and better fuel economy than its predecessor.

In overdrive, climbing ability and trailer towing capabilities were easily comparable to the 5.2-litre engine. On steeper grades, performance was actually improved as a result of the engine's broader rpm range and from careful matching of transmission gear ratios to the engine. Fuel economy improved as a result of reduced displacement and lower idle speed, coupled with greater engine and transmission efficiency.

There were several features which contributed to its brisk acceleration, pulling power and driveability. The high power output and brisk performance resulted from maximising the amount of air flow through the engine. Mounting the fuel injectors in the cylinder head (facilitated by the use of overhead camshafts), aided transient response and driveability. Intake manifold design provided optimum air flow, fast-burn combustion extracted more power from a given amount of fuel and spark plug location near the centre of the combustion chamber minimised the flame front for rapid combustion without producing potentially damaging knock.

The engine was 54lb lighter than the 5.2-litre V8 and a computer-designed water pump added 6hp to the engine output at its peak rpm. Fuel injection timing varied with operating conditions, improving cold

Also new at facelift time was the rather nice, V8 option. Not the huge 5.9L lump, but the PowerTech 4.7-litre engine still produced lots of power and torque. This is the high-output version (255bhp) seen in a 2004 special edition Platinum model.

starting and reducing the potential for start-up knock. The new V8 engine was capable of powering the new Grand Cherokee to a thundering top speed of 122mph – where permitted of course – and from 0–60mph in around eight seconds.

For UK use, fuel economy is an extremely important aspect of any engine, especially when it has eight cylinders to feed. There were several features on the new vehicle contributing to the good fuel economy of the 4.7-litre engine. Fast-burn combustion extracted more work from a given amount of fuel and with the engine itself being lighter, a figure of 22.4mpg was achieved on the extra urban cycle.

With the Grand Cherokee going ever more upmarket, NVH was a key factor. Extensive design analysis was devoted to making the 4.7-litre engine quiet. In addition, the 4.7-litre engine sound was smooth but still somehow managed to keep the glorious V8 exhaust rumble.

These qualities stemmed from two factors; first, reduction of vibration within the engine by making structures stiffer and moving parts stiffer and lighter, and secondly, eliminating noise transmission by preventing outer surfaces from resonating with noises inside the engine – reciprocating parts, valve train, camshaft drive chains, oil and water pumps, etc.

All-new automatic transmission

The all-new fully automatic, electronically controlled multi-speed 45RFE transmission made its debut in combination with the all-new 4.7-litre V8 engine. Both engine and transmission were designed and engineered simultaneously and precisely calibrated to each other, resulting in a powertrain that delivered refined power flow and increased fuel efficiency.

'This transmission is designed specifically for use in Jeep vehicles,' said David Van Raaphorst, Executive Engineer – Powertrain. 'Incorporating optimised gear ratio steps and state-of-the-art efficiency features, the 45RFE represents a new level for shift refinement, noise, vibration and harshness characteristics and durability.'

The 45RFE transmission featured unique characteristics such as a tall, 3.00:1 first gear to give

better initial acceleration. Real-time driver-adaptive gear changing fine-tuned the shift pattern to the driver, while an alternative second gear ratio gave the driver five forward ratios, enhancing driveability and performance.

During normal acceleration, second gear had a ratio of 1.67. Depending on speed and throttle position, both this gear and an alternative 1.50 second gear ratio were available for kick-down operation, making the down-shift smoother.

The 45RFE was also the only transmission in its class with a reverse gear ratio equal to the first gear ratio. While unnecessary for passenger cars, for which most competitive transmissions were developed, it was beneficial for 4x4 vehicles, which often experienced heavier loads, especially when towing.

Other innovative design features included three planetary gear sets, which combined the widest range of gear ratios available in any transmission in its class. Combined with precise step selections, this guaranteed smooth shifts, maximum power and optimal fuel efficiency under all conditions.

The 4.0-litre I-6 engine was mated to the proven, yet newly updated electronically controlled 4-speed 42RE automatic transmission.

Unsurpassed on and off-road capability

The all-new Quadra-Drive four-wheel-drive system was an industry exclusive on the 1999 Grand Cherokee. It was the first time the innovative system, a combination of the second-generation Quadra-Trac II transfer case and Vari-Lok progressive front and rear axle differentials, had been offered on any sport-utility vehicle in the world. The Quadra-Drive system had the ability to keep the Grand Cherokee going even if only one front wheel had traction.

'Quadra-Drive is a totally new concept in four-wheel-drive systems,' said David Van Raaphorst. 'This patented system provides outstanding responsiveness and traction under all driving conditions – both on and off-road – without the driver having to shift any levers or push any buttons.

'It also improves handling stability in wet weather and on slippery roads by making maximum use of available traction during acceleration. This becomes very apparent while cornering and on tight motorway slip roads,' said Van Raaphorst.

Under normal driving conditions, the Quadra-Trac II transfer case delivered most of the power to the rear wheels. The moment a wheel lost traction, a speed variation occurred between the front and rear axle causing a gerotor pump to apply hydraulic pressure to a multi-disc clutch-pack sending power to the front axle. This system allowed the vehicle to maintain traction and control seamlessly and within fractions of a second.

As in all Jeep vehicles, the Quadra-Trac II transfer case included a low range for off-road operation. Selecting low range gave a torque multiplication ratio of 2.72.

Incorporating the US industry's first speed-sensing torque transfer front differential, Vari-Lok provided a major improvement in wheel traction compared with existing four-wheel-drive systems. Under conditions in which opposite wheels are on surfaces with widely different friction characteristics, Vari-Lok delivered far more torque to the wheel on the higher traction surface than was possible with conventional limited-slip systems.

The gerotor pump incorporated in the Vari-Lok differential was conceptually the same as that used in the Quadra-Trac II transfer case. Its operation was virtually transparent to the driver, but the Grand Cherokee's ability to maintain headway and control under low-traction conditions, both on and off road was very evident.

Power transfer in a Vari-Lok differential was proportional to wheel speed difference rather than torque difference, typical in most mechanical limited-slip systems.

Response of the gerotor pump could be precisely tuned to driving conditions, enabling the use of this advanced system in the front axle as well as the rear, which was an industry breakthrough.

'Four-wheel-drive leadership through off-road capability is a hallmark of every Jeep vehicle,' said Craig Winn, General Manager of the Jeep Platform Team. 'The 1999 Grand Cherokee retains and improves upon its predecessor's unsurpassed off-road capability. This has been proven on the Rubicon Trail through the Sierra Nevada mountains, arguably one of the toughest challenges for any sport-utility vehicle and a prerequisite for all Jeep vehicles.'

At introduction from the spring of 1999, all-new Grand Cherokees had the Quadra Trac II system as standard. Quadra Drive was introduced during the late summer of 1999.

Special features for Europe

Jeep engineers in the USA recognised that European Grand Cherokee drivers were as interested in the 'sport' as they were in the 'utility'. As a result, several features unique to the European model were incorporated especially, including:

More signs of automotive progress – satellite navigation is now optional (standard on some models). This unit is all-of-a-piece containing the satnav, radio and CD and is, happily, easy to use.

- Steering gear and suspension uniquely tuned for high-speed handling
- Air-foil windscreen wipers for high-speed performance
- Unique tyres which allowed a top speed of 125mph and contributed to better handling and shorter braking distances
- Headlamps with a brighter, wider beam pattern and headlamp levelling
- RDS stereo radio/cassette as standard
- Radio antenna located in rear quarter glass on Limited model
- Unique stitch design on the seats and power fold away mirrors

'The all-new Grand Cherokee once again reaffirms the classic American design of Jeep, innovation and leadership in four-wheel-drive vehicles in the UK, Europe and world-wide,' said Richard Mackay, Managing Director of Chrysler Jeep Imports UK. 'With its new powertrains and the most sophisticated four-wheel-drive system in the world, we believe the new Grand Cherokee will further distance itself from the growing group of imitators.

'The new Grand Cherokee is also the most luxurious Jeep ever, offering a host of features and appointments comparable to the leading European premium level cars,' continued Mackay. 'In fact, today, with the current Grand Cherokee we have already become a solid E segment competitor by drawing customers out of this premium saloon segment.'

Nevertheless, Jeep ensured that the new car had all the off-road abilities of its forebears. So even if some Jeep owners never take their vehicle off-road, they know they have the legendary Jeep four-wheel-drive capability anywhere they go – and ownership in the legendary brand that started it all.

Equipment
The 4.7 V8 Limited had an equipment list a mile long. As well as the usual electric windows, central locking, the two models had two key fobs with independent memory settings, ABS anti-lock braking, side impact protection guards, air conditioning (infrared dual-zone climate control), easy-exit driver's seat, Agate or Camel leather trim, 10-way power-adjustable front seats (with two memory settings for driver's side), 180-watt RDS radio/cassette with eight speakers, and steering wheel-mounted controls.

Security was being taken ever more seriously, with a Thatcham Category 1, rolling code alarm/immobiliser being fitted as well as a visible VIN on the dashboard, radio antenna in the rear quarter window (which inhibited vandalism), and locking wheel nuts.

The 4.0 Limited fared almost as well, receiving everything that the bigger-engined model did except that the electric sunroof was an option and the 10-disc CD autochanger wasn't available. So owners didn't exactly have to rough it!

Word soon got out that the new Grand was the vehicle to be seen in and at the Earls Court London Motor Show, top girl band All Saints happily (and why not?!) collected the keys to a quartet of 4.7 V8 models.

Five alive – the new diesel engine
It was November 1999 before the much-vaunted and long-awaited new 3.1-litre five-cylinder turbo diesel engine arrived. Once more built by VM Motori in Cento, Italy, it was claimed to be brand-new, but it actually shared bore, stroke, and most moving parts with its predecessor, although it drove a new crankshaft mounted in a new block.

The significance of the new diesel engine was confirmed by Dick Winter, General Manager – International Product Planning, who commented: 'Diesel engines have been powering Grand Cherokee's success in international markets. One third of all previous-model Grand Cherokees sold outside of North America have been equipped with a diesel engine and we expect this to increase with the new vehicle and the new engine.'

The diesel engine air induction system was the mirror image of that used by the petrol engines. The new location reduced the length of the turbocharger inlet duct and as in the past, additional ducts routed air flow from the turbocharger to the intercooler, which was in front of the radiator, and back to the intake manifold.

This resulted in an increase in engine power of 25hp and 62lb ft of additional torque. The new Grand Cherokee could tow trailers of up to 3,500kg, an improvement of 1,200kg over the 2.5-litre turbo diesel, as well as providing more acceleration, load carrying and towing capacity than its predecessor. As on the petrol engine, it had electronically controlled fuel

> ### DID YOU KNOW?
>
> Cherokee diesels have always had a European flavour; early American Cherokees used a Renault turbo unit before it gave way to the Italian VM, as used in the UK. This was also used in the early Grand Cherokees and eventually, both models switched to Mercedes-Benz diesel power plants.

injection operated by an electronic accelerator control system for fast response and low emissions ('drive by wire').

To minimise interior noise and vibration, the diesel powerplant assembly (engine, transmission, and transfer case) included a set of interconnecting steel struts similar to those used with the 4.0-litre petrol engine. The struts increased the natural vibration frequency of the assembly, removing a source of annoying vibration. A new direct-mount air-conditioning compressor and compact alternator and power-steering brackets gave each of these engine accessories a high natural frequency, avoiding added vibration input to the powertrain mounts. A single serpentine belt with automatic tensioner drove all engine-mounted accessories, reducing peak bearing loads for quieter operation.

Importantly, the 1999 Grand Cherokee was the first turbo diesel-powered Jeep vehicle with automatic transmission as standard (with no manual option), which reaffirmed the upscale positioning of the vehicle in international markets. 'The automatic transmission better meets the needs of international customers in this segment,' said Winter. The 3.1-litre I-5 turbo diesel engine was combined with an electronically controlled four-speed automatic transmission, a re-engineered version of the 44RE 'box.

Frugal by name ...

To emphasise the frugal nature of the new engine, Jeep's John Taylor drove from the Dover HQ to the north west of Scotland – on a single tank of fuel. Travelling 735 miles at an average of 43mph – in a large, heavy off-roader with an automatic gearbox – certainly made a point. Coinciding with this fuel economy exercise, the Jeep Grand Cherokee passed the two million production milestone in the USA. The achievement was marked by a ceremony when the keys to the two millionth car to be built at DaimlerChrysler's Jefferson-North assembly plant were presented to the proud owner of the vehicle by Robert Eaton, Chairman of DaimlerChrysler.

Aside from collecting yet another pile of silverware from various awards ceremonies, things were fairly quiet in 2000 – until it got to September, when the company announced some price changes: they were going down! The top-of-the-range V8 fell from £34,995 to £30,995, the diesel 3.1 TD dropped by £3,000 to £27,995 and the 4.0 petrol was reduced by £2,000 to £27,995. The official comment was that the reductions

reflected a total commitment to keep Jeep strong in some of the most competitive vehicle sectors in the UK market. Whatever, knocking £4,000 off any vehicle certainly isn't going to do its sales much harm.

A new diesel engine

For 2002, the very big news for Grand Cherokee fanciers was the introduction of a brand-new 2.7 CRD diesel engine. The merger of Daimler and Chrysler (henceforth DaimlerChrysler) gave access to the Mercedes/Bosch-developed common rail engine. Common rail technology means that fuel is delivered to each cylinder via a high-pressure pump along a single line, hence the term 'common rail'. This ensures diesel fuel is injected at precisely the right moment and at exactly the right pressure for perfect combustion and unsurpassed levels of diesel engine refinement. The benefits are better performance, improved fuel consumption, reduced emissions and quieter running.

Another improvement for the oil-burning Grand was the change from the previous four-speed automatic gearbox to a new, five-speed auto which had better-spaced ratios and a faster, smoother shift than its predecessor. Quadra-Trac 11 4WD was fitted as standard to 2.7 CRD models. Add all the factors up and you get some impressive performance: 0–60mph came up in 11 seconds with a top speed of 120mph while being very economical – 34.9mpg (extra urban), 22.6mpg (urban) and 29.1mpg (combined cycle).

The Mercedes-sourced 2.7 CRD diesel engine made its debut in 2002 and proved to be very effective.

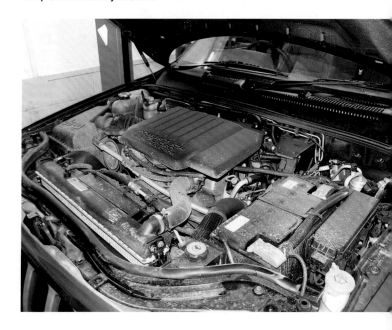

Grand Cherokee Overland

At the same time as the company was pushing the new economical diesel engine, it also launched the Overland, a version aimed fairly and squarely at drivers wanting performance first. It was based on the V8 Limited model and powered by a high-output version of the 4.7-litre engine, producing 255bhp, which equated to 16 per cent more power and 8 per cent more torque than any other production Jeep. The 0–62mph time of just over eight seconds was enough to embarrass many hot-hatches as was the top speed of almost 130mph. Numerous enhancements to the Grand Cherokee's impressive list of equipment included unique five-spoke alloy wheels, full off-road protective skid plates and rock rails, and bespoke paint: Patriot Blue, Silverstone, Onyx Green and Graphite. The interior was enhanced by specially made leather/suede seats, real redwood burl dashboard and steering wheel, and a 10-disc CD autochanger linked to a single CD radio/cassette player and eight-speaker system.

Also in 2002, the top-of-the-range Overland was launched, with the 4.7L V8 HO engine. A measure of the importance of diesels in the UK was that a year later, the same spec vehicle was available with the 2.7 CRD power plant.

At £33,995, Jeep's new range topper was the company's most expensive Grand Cherokee then on the market and yet it was, on average, £18,500 less than similar luxury 4x4s such as the Range Rover, BMW X5 and Mercedes M-Class.

At this point, the Grand Cherokee line-up spanned 2.7CRD, 4-litre and 4.7-litre V8 Limited and 4.7-litre V8 Overland models, with prices ranging from £27,999 to £33,995.

For 2003, the Grand Cherokee was offered in two new exterior colours: Bright Silver Metallic and Brilliant Black Crystal Pearl Coat. The model-year also included a host of more technical improvements, including reduced-pressure shocks for improvements in overall ride comfort and reduced brake pedal effort, allowing shorter stopping distances (this was achieved by increasing the master cylinder output pressure for a lighter brake pedal feel). Standard multi-stage driver and passenger front airbags were designed to deploy at different levels depending on the severity of the impact, while ceiling-mounted side curtain airbags were standard fitment, offering additional head protection for both front and rear passengers.

The new Grand Cherokee also offered rain-sensing front wipers which were, happily, switched to give the driver some choice. When the windscreen wiper control

is turned to 'auto', the wiper system automatically activates when it rains and adjusts its speed according to the severity of the rain.

The first new model to benefit from these changes was the 2.7 CRD Overland (previously only available with a 4.7-litre V8 petrol engine). Already available in the Limited versions, it produced 161bhp and 295lb ft of torque and came paired with five-speed automatic transmission and Quadra-Drive 4WD. Fuel consumption of the Grand Cherokee 2.7 CRD was an impressive 29.1mpg on the combined cycle. Externally, the Overland CRD was distinguished by unique machined-rim five-spoke 17-inch aluminium alloy wheels, body-colour exterior fascia panels and grille and rock rails to protect the sills. Inside, extra equipment included a power sunroof, 10-disc CD changer with remote control, unique suede and leather seat trim, 10-way powered and heated front seats, and

real redwood burr wood trim on the instrument panel, centre console, upper door trims and upper part of the steering wheel. It had an OTR price of £31,495 and retained the three-year, 60,000-mile warranty, roadside assistance and seven-year, unlimited-mile anti-corrosion guarantee.

The Grand was upgraded for the 2004 model year, receiving minor external changes such as the addition of vertical grille bars, new front driving lamps and new door mirrors, which not only looked good but further reduced wind noise. A new paint finish was added to the options list: Deep Lava Red. Prices stayed the same as in 2003, viz.

4.0 Limited	£27,995
2.7 CRD Limited	£29,500
4.7 V8 Limited	£31,000
2.7 CRD Overland	£31,500
4.7 V8 HO Overland	£34,000

In October, yet another limited edition appeared, the Grand Cherokee Stealth. Again it was based on the

Minor surgery for the 2004 model meant minor external changes such as the addition of vertical grille bars, new front driving lamps and new door mirrors.

This 2003 Stealth looks as if it means business. Powered by the 2.7-litre CRD diesel engine, the Startech Monostar III alloy wheels shod with 255/55 R18 tyres, Brilliant Black metallic paint and darkened rear privacy glass, give it a certain air of menace. It was good value, too.

punchy 2.7-litre CRD diesel engine and distinguished by the addition of Startech Monostar III alloy wheels and 255/55 R18 tyres, Brilliant Black Metallic paint and darkened rear privacy glass. With an OTR price of £30,995, buyers got £1,900 of extras for an extra £600 over the standard vehicle.

In March, the entry-level Grand Cherokee Sport was launched. It featured a 4.0-litre petrol engine (with a 2.7-litre CRD option) and had air conditioning, six-way power adjustable cloth seats, front fog lamps, 16-inch alloy wheels and single CD/radio as standard fitments. The 4.0-litre petrol engine special edition cost £24,995 and the 2.7 CRD £26,695. Exterior colours were limited

to Black, Metallic Silver and Metallic Patriot Blue (the latter two options adding £400 to the price).

On 1 October, two more Grand Cherokee special editions were launched. The new top of the heap was the Platinum, based on the existing Overland model it was available with either the 2.7 CRD or 4.7-litre V8 high-output petrol engine. It came loaded up with satnav, rear-park assist, metallic paint, 17-inch Rogue Platinum alloy wheels, 10-disc autochanger/radio with steering wheel controls, sunroof, air conditioning (including climate control) and black leather interior. Outside, it had a chrome grille, matt black rock rails and black tinted windows.

The Limited XS model was based on the Limited version and came with the same choice of engines as the Platinum. In addition, it featured metallic paint, satnav, rear-park assist, 17-inch Rogue alloy wheels, single CD/radio with steering wheel controls, sunroof, air conditioning with climate control, leather interior and chrome rock rails.

Simon Elliott, Managing Director of Chrysler and Jeep in the UK, said: 'The Grand Cherokee, which achieved this year's 'World's best off-roader' award from *4x4* magazine, offers outstanding four-wheel drive capability, which you can use either off-road or in every day driving conditions. These two new special editions make the Grand Cherokee even better value for money, with rear park assist and satnav as standard.'

DID YOU KNOW?

American vehicles have always been noted for their high level of specification as standard. By the time of the launch of the Grand Cherokee Platinum, the options list was virtually non-existent, comprising just two items: an electric sunroof and a luggage cover.

The pricing structure was:

Grand Cherokee Platinum 4.7 V8 HO	£35,995
Grand Cherokee Platinum 2.7 CRD	£33,995
Grand Cherokee Limited XS 4.7 V8	£33,715
Grand Cherokee Limited XS 2.7 CRD	£32,415

The 2004 special edition Platinum made best use of black, with tinted rear windows and ... gorgeous black leather trim with contrasting ivory piping.

Grand Cherokee Sport 2.7 CRD	£26,695
Grand Cherokee Sport 4.0	£24,995

Looking ahead – the Grand Cherokee 2005

At the time of publication, production of the new Grand Cherokee had already begun at the Jefferson North Assembly Plant in Detroit. Production for markets outside North America was scheduled for the first quarter of 2005 at the Magna Steyr Assembly Plant in Graz, Austria, but delivery to the UK hadn't started, and this was expected to be June/July 2005. However, there was plenty of information available to let us know what to expect, notably from the launch at the 2004 New York Motor Show.

From head-on, the new vehicle is unmistakably a Grand Cherokee. The twin headlamps make a statement and the way they are recessed into the bonnet has echoes of the current Cherokee model.

'Jeep continues to be the only American brand dedicated solely to the sport-utility market,' said Jeff Bell, Chrysler Group Vice President – Jeep. 'Customers expect every Jeep to set the standard for off-road capability, and the all-new Jeep Grand Cherokee will not disappoint. What is unexpected is that the Jeep Grand Cherokee will also be the leader in on-road performance excitement.' Brave words, so let's see what we've been promised.

New style outside and in

From the outside the signature seven-slot grille is flanked by twin round high-performance halogen headlamps, both of which are eased into the bonnet edge in a similar way to the smaller Cherokee and emphasise the family resemblance. A proportionally

longer hood and greater distance between the centre of the front axle and base of the windshield visually create a more powerful image. The overall design improves vehicle aerodynamics and fuel economy. Larger tail lamps at the rear feature red and clear lenses for an upmarket appearance.

Inside, it is quite clear that Jeep has targeted both the Series 3 Land Rover Discovery and Range Rover models, it having a distinctly top-end feel. Seat contours are precise and ergonomic with increased seat track travel and headroom to make the interior feel more spacious. The elegant instrument panel design offers a high degree of precision and control and in the cargo area, features such as a reversible load floor panel enhance versatility and storage. New premium amenities – including GPS navigation radio,

rear-seat DVD, Boston Acoustics audio, Uconnect Bluetooth hands-free communication system, Smart Beam and rear-park assist – will also be available.

Engine line-up

We can't be certain that the UK will get the 5.7-litre, Hemi V8 engine – shame! The Jeep Grand Cherokee was the first SUV to offer the multi-displacement system (MDS) which deactivates half the cylinders during cruising and light acceleration, which increases fuel economy by up to 20 per cent. Ninety per cent of peak torque was available from 2,400rpm to 5,100rpm for excellent performance while trailer towing, travelling

The rear too couldn't be much else other than a Grand, although it's decidedly less fussy and has more conventional lamp clusters.

The stylish interior was clearly aimed at such top-end opposition as the BMW X5, Range Rover and Discovery.

off-road as well as city and highway driving. A sophisticated electronic throttle control (ETC) system tailors throttle response to pedal movement based on operating conditions, and maintains a more consistent vehicle speed on rolling grades when cruise control is active than the former mechanical throttle control system.

The 4-litre, straight-six engine replaces a 3.7-litre SOHC V6 as in the existing Cherokee model, but the 4.7-litre SOHC V8 engine continues to be available.

Four-wheel-drive systems
Three new full-time four-wheel-drive systems are available. Quadra-Trac I utilises the NV140 single-speed

transfer case to provide convenient full-time four-wheel drive with no transfer case lever to shift, attracting the sort of buyer who wants the facilities without input. Quadra-Trac II incorporates the new NV245 transfer case which provides full-time active four-wheel drive, that anticipates and prevents wheel slip for optimum traction during a wide range of conditions. The NV245 also includes electronic shift with a true low-range gear and a neutral position, for towing behind another vehicle.

Quadra-Drive II is the top of the heap, using electronic limited slip differentials (ELSD) to give customers the ultimate in off-road capability. ELSD replaces the Vari-Lock progressive axles used on the previous Quadra-Drive system for even quicker response to changing conditions and greater torque capacity.

Shifting gears

An all-new five-speed automatic transmission offers smooth shifts and optimum fuel economy with the 3.7-litre V6. The carryover 545RFE five-speed automatic transmission used with the 4.7-litre V8 and 5.7-litre V8 HEMI has been refined for higher-quality shifts while increasing the Grand Cherokee's maximum towing capacity.

Both featured electronic range select (ERS) driver interactive shift control for the first time on Grand Cherokee. The shifter provides fully automated shifting when in the 'drive' position, or the driver can select each gear manually by simply moving the shifter left or right from the 'drive' position. This gave the driver control to precisely match any on-road or off-road driving requirement. A new stamped steel skid plate is mounted on the transmission cross-member and fuel tank to provide off-road protection to the transfer case.

Suspension

At the front is an all-new independent front suspension designed to give more precision and control with more precise steering while also reducing vehicle weight.

The front three-quarter view shows that the designers have got it right again, retaining shades of the previous model and of the two Cherokees as well. The trademark stretched trapezoidal wheelarches blend neatly into the wings and, of course, there's that famous grille.

Front suspension wheel travel is increased by 13 per cent over the previous car, and a turning diameter of 37.1ft is an improvement over the current Grand Cherokee to provide more nimble handling. The new five-link rear suspension geometry, including a track bar, also improves lateral stiffness to match that of the front suspension for optimum handling.

Also offered for the first time, electronic stability program (ESP) aids the driver in maintaining vehicle directional stability in severe driving manoeuvres on any type of surface. Using signals from sensors throughout the vehicle, the system determines the appropriate brake and throttle adjustments for directional stability.

The new rack-and-pinion steering system imparts a more precise steering feel through fewer linkages than a recirculating ball steering system, even with a 2.5in increase in track.

Chapter Four

Let's off-road!

Please note that all photographs showing vehicles off road were taken either on official off-road routes, purpose-made off-road centres, or on private land with the owner's permission.

It's a fact – albeit a sad one – that most Jeeps never see anything more muddy than the school playing field. What a waste, when you have one of the most capable

Left: A Series 2 Cherokee cresting what could loosely be called a 'rise'; now is not the time for a crisis of confidence! (Nick Dimbleby)

off-road vehicles in the world at your right foot.

Off-road driving is a whole load of fun and, compared with most other forms of motor 'sport' is extremely safe. As is often said, it's a great adrenaline rush at just 2mph! But the technique of driving without tarmac under the wheels is absolutely nothing at all like normal

Below: It is wise to think ahead and carry an emergency kit with you. This is what a professional carries, which is a little excessive for mild green-laning. The equipment carried also includes a winch at the rear and ... (Nick Dimbleby)

... at the front, all the better for getting out of sticky situations. Winching is an art in itself and shouldn't be attempted by the unskilled. (Nick Dimbleby)

Once the bug has bitten, this is the sort of thing it does to you! This early Cherokee has been lifted and the ground clearance further increased by fitting massive off-road tyres, the full extent of which ...

driving, and to a great extent, you have to undo much of what you have learned and take on board some weird and wonderful new techniques. You are heartily recommended to try at least one day at a specialist training course, where you can learn the new skills required to be safe off-road. More importantly, perhaps, this will give you an insight into bad-condition driving-control required for driving in snow etc.

You can go off-roading with a number of specialist driving schools which cater for all manner of off-roaders or with the folks who sell the Jeep itself (currently DaimlerChrysler). They organise training days which take place at various sites across the country. Jeep Skills Days have trained instructors who make sure you understand exactly how to get the best from your very capable vehicle. Numbers are limited, to ensure the best levels of tuition, and all cars are fitted with two-way radio for extra driver reassurance.

Alternatively, you can go the whole hog and attend a Privilege Event. These are off-roading based adventures held world-wide and in 2004 spanned Dartmoor, Ireland, The Pyrenees and Aviemore in Scotland, lasting between three and eight days. These also include various other activities, such as clay pigeon shooting, fly fishing and visits to whisky distilleries! It is well to bear in mind though, that driving off-road isn't solely about having fun. You will learn just how capable your car really is and this is something that simply can't be explained: you have to experience it. This will give much more justifiable confidence in the vehicle and the way you drive it. More importantly, when faced with a natural hazard, such as deep snow, you will know exactly what to do to get through it.

Where to get off road

Despite the government's best efforts (aided and abetted by many pressure groups with universally selfish motives), there are still plenty of green lanes suitable for legal off-roading. However, it is vital that

... is clearly illustrated here. No problem with access to the front axle and suspension, then!

you check and *double-check* that the lanes you use are specified for your use – it is irresponsible to give ammunition to the 'we-want-the-countryside-for-ourselves' brigade. You'll need the very latest, large-scale Ordnance Survey maps but even they need to be checked as changes made to lanes can take some years to appear in print. (At the time of writing, the future of vehicular access to green lanes was still in doubt, and subsequent legislation may affect your right to do this.)

By far the best way to approach the subject is to join a club – either a general 4 x 4 club or one specifically

for Jeep vehicles. Most have officers who deal with green-laning issues and stay in touch with the local councils to keep tabs on which lanes are officially open to vehicles and which aren't. It also gives you the opportunity to take part in an organised drive which not only adds a pleasant social element to the day, but also means that there's someone to help out should you get it all wrong.

And how would you like to have an interesting day's green-laning, meet lots of like-minded folk and do something for the environment? Well, with the cost of scrapping old vehicles being down to the owner, more and more old wrecks are being dumped in our green and pleasant land. Many clubs are making a point of

Water acts like a magnet to off-roaders and is great fun, given a little common sense. Driving down a shallow stream like this isn't difficult, as long as you're sure there are no nasty hidden boulders or holes to trap the unwary.

clearing lanes not only of rotten old cars (dangerous in themselves of course) but also of many years of neglect in terms of waist-high undergrowth, fallen trees and household rubbish. This clearly benefits everyone who wants to use the lane and is one in the eye for certain factions who want to have sole access to such lanes – which have been available to large, wheeled vehicles for many hundreds of years – but who seem to be curiously missing when such maintenance work is required …

Where the tarmac ends …

The Cherokee – any model – is more or less ready to go, with tyres being probably the most important limiting factor. For standard green-laning or a reasonable off-road course, you won't need to do anything much to your car. However, remember that extras such as side steps and a towing bracket will limit your ground clearance and of course the front spoiler

Where it's deeper much more care is required to prevent water getting into the air intake (and from there into the engine), or swirling round the rear of the car and blocking the exhaust (which can lead to 'hydraulicing' and a wrecked engine). Enter such depths slowly, having checked the route beforehand, and build up speed to produce a bow wave just around bumper height, as here. Keeping the speed even will prevent accidents and vehicle damage.

(and with its lights) is also directly in the firing line. It's the driver that needs the most preparation and it is advisable to take at least some off-road training before you venture out solo. Remember also, that green lanes are public roads and that you and your passengers should wear seat belts at all times. Even on a private site, this is an essential safety measure – imagine up-ending your Jeep *without* seat belts!

Be prepared

It is definitely *not* recommended to go off-roading alone for obvious safety reasons, and don't consider it unless your car is in top condition with all fluid levels checked and it is generally behaving perfectly. Take suitable footwear, and as mud is all but guaranteed, this means tough boots and/or wellies. It's a wise move to invest in a set of seat covers, at least for the front seats, as mud gets absolutely everywhere especially if you become involved in helping to pull out a stuck vehicle.

Always take a first-aid kit with you and a 12v tyre-inflator is very useful, as it means you can lower the tyre pressures when required, knowing they can be returned to the original figures when driving home. CB radio or two-way walkie-talkies are handy tools to have and your mobile phone should be to hand, fully charged of course. A good torch (well-charged or with

spare batteries) is a must, especially in the winter months when days are much shorter.

Carry something in the way of sustenance (a vacuum flask with a hot drink, sandwiches, chocolate etc.) and always make sure you have a full tank of fuel before you start – remember that off-roading can reduce your typical mpg by 50 per cent or more. It also pays to carry a spare gallon of fuel, suitably strapped down.

Empty the car of non-essential contents and tie everything down that is likely to fly around as the car goes over very uneven surfaces and up and down steep inclines.

If you're green-laning, you will need an Ordnance Survey map (Landranger 1:50,000) relating to the area you're in. If you have satellite navigation (satnav) on board or can borrow a portable system, then so much the better. A good quality tow rope won't go amiss – talk to an off-roading specialist to get the best rope for your purposes and particular vehicle; the sort of thing you get for towing a Nissan Micra down the motorway is specifically not what you want! Your usual tool kit is a must as is a spade (not a shovel). A couple of bin liners can be used to keep your muddy boots in on the drive back, a muddy tow rope if it has been used and, of course, any rubbish you create (such as sandwich wrappers, empty cans etc.).

Oh, and don't forget your camera – not only will you get to see some beautiful parts of the countryside not normally available to mere mortals, you'll probably have some pretty wild stories about crossing rivers and conquering mountains which will be all the more convincing if you have photographic proof to back them up!

When you come back onto metalled roads, be aware that lots of mud and grit in the wheels, steering and brakes will do them no good at all. Make sure they work efficiently and take the first opportunity you can to blast them clean. It's good reason to buy a pressure washer, because no garage forecourt will want you using theirs and clogging up the drains with half a ton of mud!

Ground clearance

Make sure you understand and know exactly what your vehicle is capable of. Regardless of your school maths results, there are three angles you need to know, as follows:

The *approach angle* is that between your car and an incline. You need to make sure that your front wheels touch the hill before your front spoiler.

Or of course, you could just avoid the water altogether by taking to the bank!

The *ramp angle* defines the side steepness of a hill – you don't want to get your Cherokee beached on its belly.

The *departure angle* is the opposite of the approach angle and relates to the angle of the hill in relation to the lower rear of the vehicle. The Cherokee isn't bad in this area, but a towing bracket seriously inhibits its performance.

Of course, the Grand Cherokee models are longer overall and thus lose out on some of the versatility of the smaller models. Get any of these wrong and you could damage the vehicle and put yourself (and your passengers) in danger.

The importance of tyres

All the traction in the world is useless if you have no grip, and that's the job of the tyres. All Cherokees leave the factory with road-biased tyres fitted, which are usually described as being an 80/20 balance in favour of metalled roads. They'll offer almost saloon car levels

Below: It helps to have a head for heights – a sudden attack of vertigo down a hill like this would be decidedly unpleasant.

Top left: Having all-wheel drive is only part of the equation when it comes to off-roading – or tarmac driving come to that. This Wrangler HP all-weather tyre is typical of the type used where almost all driving is done on metalled roads. It will be quieter day-to-day and give higher cornering speeds. However, it won't cope with mud or snow as well as …

Top right: … the 'AT/R' (all-terrain), which clearly has a much different tread. As the name suggests, these tyres are designed for driving regularly on muddy roads and/or in lots of water, or if you drive on roads with a less than perfect surface. It's a more aggressive design combining anti-aquaplaning performance, increased mud dispersion and off-road traction, but still not being overly noisy on-road.

Above: For some serious mud-plugging, the 'MT/R' (mud-terrain) tyre is the one to go for. It has a special block design for additional traction and grip, as well as Dura-wall technology for sidewall penetration protection. It's still legal for tarmac use, but cornering speeds will be lower and noise levels will be higher.

of comfort, grip and quiet and be quite capable when dealing with minor off-road excursions. At the other extreme, there's the 'MT' (mud-terrain) type of tyre, which has tread deep enough to swallow small children whole and which will grip in mud and snow like no road tyre would. These are designed to clear away the mud as if it wasn't there and although they can be used on metalled roads, they will compromise cornering and handling, and cabin noise levels will increase dramatically. In-between are all-terrain tyres which many drivers choose as being the perfect compromise. Another answer is to buy a set of cheap, steel wheels to use as 'slaves' for a set of serious 'MT' rubber for off-road use. If you live in a higher part of the country where bad winters are par for the course, you can do a straight swap, say November to March every year. For road/summer use the standard alloys can be put back on again along with the road tyres. It takes half an hour or less to do this change and it is well worth it. It is

advisable to have a decent torque wrench to hand if this is the route you choose – you really don't want to have three wheels on *your* wagon!

Make sure, however, that you only use road-legal tyres if you're going off road down official green lanes. Firstly, these lanes are still classed as public highways so you'd be running illegally, and secondly, really deep-treaded competition-only tyres would churn up the ground in no uncertain fashion, which is something nobody wants.

Gearing down

All Cherokees have low-range gearing as well as conventional road-biased ratios and by using that little gear lever alongside the main one, you can enter those low ratios – known by most as the low box. This gearing reduction is what makes the Jeep so useful off-road, allowing the car to travel very slowly without the need to use the clutch or brakes and is ideal for coming down steep, muddy hills where using either would result in a very unpleasant scene indeed.

General hints and tips

Steering wheel

We're always taught to grip the steering wheel firmly, but when off-roading some care is required; if your thumbs are positioned inside the wheel and the driven wheels sudden snap sideways (after getting snagged in a deep rut for example) the steering wheel will suddenly spin round, the result usually being broken thumbs!

This sort of thing also calls for some steady nerves, especially as this Cherokee has slippery wet tyres after negotiating the stream behind. Until you've done it, you simply won't believe how far over your Cherokee will drive without falling on its side, and it's not just the smaller car …

Ground work

Take the trouble to understand what's underneath your car and moreover, which bits are likely to ground first. In most cases, it's the front/rear differential casings (the bits sticking out from the axles) and as these are rather expensive to replace you really don't want to start hitting large rocks with them

Slippage

If you're in serious mud you will probably feel the wheels start to slip. Blipping the throttle, to increase and decrease the amount of torque through the wheels, several times in quick succession can often seek out the grip required. Equally, turning the steering wheel from lock to lock can have the same effect.

Look before you leap

Lurching headlong into the unknown only happens at the cinema – they don't have to pay for the repairs! Always check ahead for what might be hiding in the mud, under tall grass or in the middle of a stream.

When attempting a steep ascent, look particularly for hidden rocks or worse, tree stumps, which could throw you off line. (This sort of thing can be even worse when going downhill, as it can easily tip the car over.) It's all very well making a tricky climb, but what's over the other side? You need to know before you get there, especially as there'll be a breathtaking few seconds where all you can see is your bonnet and the sky (at which point, experienced drivers will be looking out of the side windows for their bearings). When going down hill, select the lowest gear you can and DON'T TOUCH THE PEDALS! This goes against human nature, but letting the engine braking take the strain means that you retain complete control of the vehicle. Once you brake and/or dip the clutch, you have a runaway Jeep on your hands; not nice. At a push, you might occasionally dab the brakes lightly (more usually required on automatic cars), but always, always keep off the clutch.

Tackle hills – up or down – head-on; approaching them at angle is a recipe for disaster as it only takes a slight hidden bump to lift the unloaded front of the car and send it end-over-end to the bottom.

Wading through water

Once the bug has bitten, you'll find that water has a magnetic attraction and it can be fun, given a bit of common sense. Always make sure you know what's under the water, not least that it doesn't suddenly dip to 7ft deep in the middle! Whether it's a river, a stream or a simple ford, ensure that you have a way to get out at the other side. Enter the water slowly using low range first or second gear and slowly build speed so that a bow wave (like a motor boat) is created at the front. It should be just above bumper height and you need to keep it constant. If you slow, water will start to come back at the vehicle with the real danger of getting into the exhaust pipe and causing 'hyrdaulicing' of the engine – i.e. locking it solid. Once you're back on terra firma, remember that for a few yards, you will have no

... the Grand Cherokee can cut it just as well off-road.

braking; dry the pads and discs by easing forward in low box with the foot brake applied.

A common mistake is to enter deep water with the headlamps ablaze. The sudden shock of a hot headlamp glass hitting very cold water has the obvious effect of cracking the glass.

Caring for the environment

In 2001, Chrysler Jeep was one of the founder members of Tread Lightly!, the non-profit-making organisation dedicated to promoting responsible off-roading. The common-sense guidelines mean that Jeep owners can get the most out of their car while protecting the environment. These guidelines are simple to follow, and even easier to remember thanks to the use of the mnemonic, TREAD.

T

Travel only on trails, roads, or land areas that are open to vehicles or other forms of travel. Make sure the trail you plan to use is available for your type of vehicle. Wide vehicles on narrow trails can damage both the trail and your vehicle. Cutting switchbacks or taking

Of course, it doesn't have to be wet, muddy or high to be an off-road challenge – these rocks call for no small amount of driving skill.

shortcuts can destroy vegetation and cause others to use the unauthorised route. Most trails and routes designated for 4x4 use are constructed to withstand the effects of use. Staying on these trails reduces the impacts from 4x4 vehicles.

R

Respect and be courteous to other users who also want to enjoy the lands you are using for your travels. Be considerate and honour their desire for solitude and a peaceful countryside experience. Loud motors and noisy behaviour are not acceptable and detract from a quiet outdoor setting. Give other people the space and quiet you would appreciate. Driving near or around someone's camp site is not appreciated. When driving, be especially cautious around horses or hikers. Pull off to the side of the track, shut off your engine, and let the horses or hikers pass. In and around campgrounds, be sensitive to campers' need for a peaceful atmosphere. If your exhaust silencer is not quiet, push your machine into and out of a camp ground, with the engine shut off.

E

Educate yourself by stopping and talking with land managers at their office. Or, if you see them in the field,

stop and ask questions. They can tell you what areas and routes are suitable for off-roading. Travel maps are usually available at most offices. On private lands, be sure to obtain the owner or land manager's permission to cross or use their land. As you travel the countryside, comply with trail and road signs. Honour all gates, fences and barriers that are there to protect the natural resources, wildlife and livestock.

A

Avoid sensitive areas at all times. In early spring and autumn, rain and snow typically saturate the ground making soil surfaces soft. Improper vehicle use can cause damage to vegetation and ground surface. Stay on designated roadways and trails so that new scars are not established. Especially sensitive areas susceptible to scarring are stream banks, lake shores and meadows. Cross streams only at fords where the road or trail intersects the stream. Travelling in a stream channel is unacceptable and causes damage to aquatic life. Hillside climbing may be a challenge, but once vehicle scars are established, other vehicles follow the same ruts and do long lasting damage. Rain causes further damage by washing deep gullies in tyre ruts and permanent and unsightly scars result. While operating your 4x4, be sensitive to the life-sustaining needs of wildlife and livestock. In deep snow, stay clear of game, so that vehicle noise and close proximity do not add stress to animals struggling to survive.

D

Drive and travel responsibly to protect the forests, lands and waters that you enjoy. You enjoy the outdoors for a number of good reasons, the countryside is beautiful; you have freedom to roam vast scenic areas; you see clear flowing streams and rivers; you see wild game and birds; you breathe clean air; you see and smell fragrant and colourful vegetation, trees, flowers and brush; you develop a sense of being a part of this great and expansive outdoors! These and others are reasons enough for you to do all you can to help protect the lands that mean so much to you.

Help preserve the beauty and the inspiring attributes of our lands for yourself and new generations to follow.

Note, this chapter has only covered the basic rules of driving off-road. For a in-depth study, consult specialist Haynes publications such as *The Off-Road 4-Wheel-Drive Book* by Jack Jackson.

Knowing where you are is ever more important on the UK's crowded roads and when you're off-road in the middle of nowhere, it's even more so. When you have satnav as a standard fitment, you're sorted, but if not, a portable unit such as this one from Garmin is good, not least since you can swap it from car to car.

Even more portable, is this hand-held *Sportrak Pro* from Magellan. Ideally suited to the regular off-roader, especially if hiking or mountain-biking are part of the weekend's excesses.

Choosing and buying a Jeep Cherokee

(Thanks are due to Elliot Dunmore at EDM Jeep Specialists for his assistance with this chapter.)

So, you're convinced that the Cherokee is for you? The first thing to realise is that the Cherokee is a modern-day success story and as a result, they are hardly thin on the ground. There's no shortage of choice and no reason to rush out and buy a bad one. As with most cars, membership of an owners' club is a good starting place; you'll find a fount of knowledge, a source of well cared for cars to look at and, most importantly, someone who knows the right answers to your questions. It's also a place to meet owners of like mind and from where to buy used parts and accessories.

Pre-buying checks

It's advisable to check the provenance of any car you intend to buy with one of the recognised agencies – before you pay over any money. It really doesn't matter which you choose, as long as you do. Some sellers may try to pressure a sale but remember, there are plenty of good Cherokees around and if you lose this one, there'll be another along soon. According to the AA's records, they come across a vehicle that needs further investigation every 12 seconds. A call to one of the organisations listed here will reveal such things as its presence on the stolen vehicle register, whether there is finance owing, a confirmation of the chassis and engine numbers, the vehicle colour, in which country it was originally registered, or if it has been written off at some point. The (current) cost of around £40 is nothing

Left: If mountains were meant to be climbed by mountaineers, hills were put there simply to give Jeep owners somewhere to show their car's abilities. (Nick Dimbleby)

compared with the possible loss of many thousands of pounds.

HPI Equifax
01722 413434
www.hpicheck.com

AA Used Car Data Check
0870 600 0838
www.theaa.com

RAC
0870 533 3660
www.rac.co.uk

Below: The exhaust catalyst is an expensive part to replace. This one was clearly on its way home, rattling loudly when the engine was first started. A failed cat also means a failed MoT.

Look before you leap

Lots of people just jump in and drive off when buying a car, but there's lots to do before you even turn the engine over. Start with a visual check; from across the street the Jeep should look good, sitting four-square with no obvious leaning and with no nasty oil or coolant puddles beneath it. Any model Cherokee tends to have quite a bit of street presence and it should look good – this is not everything of course, but at this point it's important; if it looks a bit down at heel, tatty and uncared for, it probably is. Unless you like pain and financial ruin, look elsewhere.

As you walk round the car, look hard at the paintwork for evidence of respraying (such as 'orange peel' effect, dull patches, slight colour mismatches etc.). Kneel down and looking right along the flanks of the car will get you some odd glances, but it will also

Left: All Jeeps are well-equipped and build-quality is good, but replacement of failed gadgets and gizmos can be expensive. If it clicks, whirrs or hums, check it carefully.

Below: You'd be very unlikely to find rust on a Jeep, but that shouldn't stop you looking under every carpet you can. This car had spent its life on the Scottish coast, pulling boats from the salt sea water – and it shows!

reveal even the slightest imperfections. All Cherokees are larger than average vehicles which, rather perversely, means they tend to get bumped and bashed in car parks more than most.

Remember that wet paintwork on any car will look good, so if it's been washed recently or it has just rained, take along a chamois to wipe it clear and show up any possible paintwork flaws.

Paperwork

If you're happy that it *looks* right, then it's on to the paperwork – note this is still before you drive the car. If the V5C (log book) isn't present, come back when it is. It's a common con-trick for it to be lost, machine-washed, eaten by the dog etc. Check the number of owners, that the description matches the vehicle (colour, number of doors etc.), the exact age and that the chassis and engine numbers tally. Does the VIN plate show signs of tampering? Be suspicious, because car thieves are irritatingly clever and giving a car a false identity (ringing) is increasingly common.

Mileage

Buying a low-mileage car seems to be the Holy Grail for many would-be owners, but there's two sides to every coin. Many Cherokees are very low mileage, mostly the larger engined petrol versions which cost the most to run. This is fine in a way, but the downside is that, by definition, such an engine must spend much of its time below full working temperature and using extra fuel, which tends to wash the protective oil from the bores. In addition, low mileage can mean that the car goes many years between services, which is a very bad thing.

A high-mileage car can often be a much better proposition, because it's spent proportionately more time at its correct operating temperature, and will almost certainly have a nice full book of service stamps. So as soon as something goes wrong – or even looks as if it might – it is sorted. Particularly with older cars, it's often better to buy on condition rather than mileage. And of course, higher miles means a lower price.

Conversions

It's not uncommon for petrol-powered Cherokees to have had an LPG conversion. Unfortunately, the UK government has been predictably lax in controlling who

A nice original-spec Mopar towing bracket like this will save you the expense of fitting one, but it also means your prospective purchase could have led a hard life. Engine, transmission, tyres and springs demand even more attention.

Front ball joints – top and bottom – fail regularly on Series 1 Cherokees. They're disproportionately expensive to replace and it's an MoT failure point. Check also the anti-roll bar drop links and cushions.

The built-in roof rails are a Cherokee speciality and can be incredibly useful. The cross bars – which should be under the seat – simply slot into place and are just as easy to remove when you've finished (in order to improve fuel economy).

can convert cars and how well they should do it. The not unexpected result is that the quality of installation varies alarmingly. An expert is a must when looking at an LPG converted petrol car. Think about where the LPG tank is sited and whether or not it will affect how you want to use it; if it is in the luggage area, it will limit the loads you can take and if under the front floors, it will limit the car's use off-road. If it's in the Grand Cherokee spare wheel well, what are you going to do about punctures?

The size of the tank(s) is important, especially if you live in an area where LPG is in limited supply. Remember that for safety reasons LPG tanks can only be filled to 80 per cent of their total capacity. If anyone tells you they've had theirs changed to take 100 per cent, do *NOT* get involved, as it makes the entire system extremely dangerous and volatile!

With a conversion of any description, check the attitude of your insurers *before you buy*. Some companies reach for the barge pole at the mere mention of the word 'conversion' but with alterations becoming more common, it is not the problem it once was. There's plenty of specialist insurers around and they understand the nature of the beast. All are likely to want at the very least an engineer's report as to the quality of installation, safety aspects and whether or not the brakes and suspension should be uprated as a result of the change.

General tips

- See the car at the buyer's house – anyone trying to sell a stolen car or a 'ringer' (a car with a false identity) will usually prefer to meet you somewhere else, or come to your house.
- Many crafty thieves park outside someone else's house and just 'happen to be outside with the car' (washing it, maybe) when you arrive, so you assume that the house is theirs. Always try to get inside the house if you can – asking to go to the loo is fair. If the seller hasn't got the house keys ('my daughter has them and has just gone to the supermarket' etc.) then be extremely wary.
- A keen owner will know where all the controls are – an 'owner' fumbling around for basics is a warning sign.
- The more paperwork, the better, especially MoT certificates, which are essential in plotting a car's true mileage.

The buyer's tool kit

- Torch which lights up awkward nooks and crannies and makes you look like a serious buyer.
- Chamois leather to wipe away a recent rinse or rain shower.
- Mat or carpet to kneel on when looking underneath.

- Magnet – to check that what should be steel isn't rust or filler.
- List of salient questions and points.
- Your own detailed list of what the standard specification should be.
- Assistant, preferably knowledgeable, who will also distract the seller so you can concentrate on thorough checking.
- Clipboard and notepad, to keep track of your thoughts – it will also make you look clued-up.
- A good idea of typical prices in your area – they vary across the country.

When to buy

Plan your ownership carefully; study what there is and what you want. Ideally, buy your car in the summer months for five main reasons:

1. There's more light and it means you can view with some confidence in the evenings.
2. It is (or should be …) warmer, so you'll be more likely to take your time and thus spot potential problem areas.
3. It is (or should be …) dryer and thus you'll be more inclined to grovel around on the floor looking for underbody damage, oil leaks, rust and rot, worn bushes etc.
4. Psychologically, people buy cabrios and sports cars in the summer and anything with 4WD in the winter. It follows that the prices of any 4WD vehicle will be more during the winter months and less in the summer – which is the time to buy your Cherokee.
5. If the worst happens and you do buy a car that requires work, it's less hardship sorting it out when you're not knee-deep in snow and fighting a −7° wind-chill factor.

Jeep Cherokee buying checklist

This check list should be used as a basic guide in conjunction with the more detailed sections in this chapter.

Location, location, location

Try to view at owner's home. Meeting in car parks etc. is suspicious – the car may be stolen. Check its regular parking place for signs of oil/coolant leaks.

Is the log book (V5C) present?

STOP NOW! Do not buy a Jeep of any hue without seeing the V5C (or V5 up to December 2003; invalid from 1 July 2005). Don't accept that it was swallowed by the dog or eaten by the washing machine.

Check the V5C details

Make sure everything checks out – name/address, number of owners, engine, chassis and VIN number etc. Any discrepancies

It's worth checking the cross bars because some owners get carried away when loading up and damage them – look at the damage in the centre of this rear bar.

should be ironed out before continuing. Use the 'numbers' appendix to make sure it is the correct model and hasn't been doctored in some way.

Check alloy wheels carefully for signs of kerbing or salt corrosion.

Is there at least some service history, invoices etc.?

Some invoices quote a mileage, so check to see if it makes sense. Older cars probably won't be dealer-serviced but enthusiasts tend to keep every single invoice for parts replaced and service items bought; the less there is, the more you should worry.

Are there MoT certificates?

Again, enthusiasts hoard these and if present, they give some idea of the true mileage. Ensure that the mileages tally. An apparently enthusiast-owned Cherokee with no previous MoTs should strike a discord – proceed with caution.

Viewing
Wet, wet, wet

Is it raining or has it rained recently? Has the car just been washed? Bear this in mind – water makes any car's paintwork look better than it is. Take a chamois to wipe the surface clean so you can see what lies beneath.

Are you viewing in fading light?

You really can't inspect a car properly in the dark or half-light. OK, you can get a general impression of a car as dusk falls, but don't buy before you've had a thorough, daylight inspection.

Look hard all around the car

Check along its flanks for accident damage. Inside boot and engine bay for minor bumps – check for signs of overspray etc.

When inspecting the tyres, remember that later, lower-profile tyres are often 'handed' and can only be fitted on one side of the vehicle. They're more expensive and can create hassles when you want to swap them round. All such tyres are clearly marked, as here.

Look in the engine bay

Check that the oil and coolant levels are correct – if they're not, it points to inconsistent maintenance and a slap-happy owner. Dirty oil or brown coolant are worrying signs as are oil leaks and a generally scruffy bay.

Look under the car

Check for oil leaks from engine, transmission or dampers – learn the difference between a gentle weep and an expensive drip. Look under wheelarches and along sills for damage or rust. Check exhaust condition.

Wheels and tyres

Check wheels for serious damage – expect minor scuffs. Check tyres for legal tread, uneven patterns, sidewall damage etc. Look at brake discs and pads through wheels. Damaged and/or scored discs and badly worn pads mean no test drive until replaced. You should know the cost of replacements.

Interior trim

Check condition is commensurate with mileage. Cherokee trim is always good quality and hard-wearing and it is quite possible to 'clock' a high-mileage car without it looking amiss.

Interior functions

Make sure everything electrical works, especially expensive kit such as air conditioning.

Driving
Start the car

It should start easily and idle cleanly straight away – if not, there could be fuel-injection or electronic problems.

Drive the car if possible on a selection of road surfaces

Check all gears engage and stay there. Listen for untoward noises from engine/suspension.

Braking

Brakes should stop the car quickly and in a straight line. Check ABS light operation (where fitted) – incorrect function is an MoT failure point.

After the test drive

Let the engine idle for a few minutes then blip the throttle – a puff of blue smoke indicates engine wear and lots of expense.

Check the provenance

Use HPI, AA, RAC or any company offering similar facilities. The current cost of around £40 could save you many thousands. This essential phone call can reveal if the car has been stolen, written-off, still has finance against it etc., even against a changed 'personal' numberplate.

The deal

Like in an auction, set your budget beforehand and stick to it. Know replacement prices and use them as a lever to get to your price. Offset against any spares included in the deal.

The choice

The car you buy has to be the right one for you at the right price. Never forget that there are thousands of Cherokees for sale now. If you're not totally sure, walk away and find another.

Insurance

Shop around is the obvious advice. Check out the adverts in the specialist 4 x 4 magazines or on the Internet. You can cut your costs by opting for a limited-mileage policy, especially as many Cherokees are used as second cars. If you're intending to off-road your car, check the policy small print as some will exclude it. Remember also that when driving on an official green-lane, you are technically still on a public highway, so your insurance *must* be valid. Make sure you're specific about what your car has fitted so there can be no squabbling in the event of a prang. This applies to major things including engine conversions, but also to less obvious items such as bull bars.

Paying the price

The various buying guides will give you a good starting point as to what is a good price and what isn't, although prices will vary with the area you're in. Buying from a Jeep dealer means you pay a premium but you should get a comprehensive warranty to ease the financial pain. However, the franchises only handle younger/low-mileage cars, and you're unlikely to find all but the very best early Cherokees there. There are various specialist dealers, some of which are reputable but equally, there's plenty of cowboys ready to lasso the unwary. Take your time, check around and look for personal recommendations if you can. Buying privately is a cheaper way still to buy a car, but of course, you've no warranty and, as long as the car wasn't falsely described, no comeback at all. Knowing your onions will prevent the tears or alternatively, take someone who does.

This applies even more so to the very cheapest way to buy – at an auction. Buying at a general sale is OK, but limits your options. Probably the best choice is a specialist 4x4 auction, such as those at Brightwells in

Buying from a Jeep franchised dealer means you'll be buying a younger car and paying more than from a specialist dealer or privately. What you will get in return is a good warranty and – hopefully – a better car.

Leominster. By definition, it's the buying method with the most risk, but the savings are enormous and usually mean that you will have a large cash safety net to soak up any possible problems. Inspection time is limited and you're unlikely to be able to drive the cars, although some will allow the engine to be started. You'll need to have your cash or card ready to pay and have some insurance sorted so you can drive home – unless you trailer it. Warranty is typically just one hour and will cover only major problems – a five-speed gearbox which will only select three gears for example. The two major rules are simple: know your stuff or take someone with you who does, and set a price limit before the auction starts – *and stick to it*!

What to buy – choosing the right model

The first choice is one of age – the car, that is. At the time of writing, even the oldest Series 2 Cherokees were only just out of warranty (and not even that if it had been extended). And the earliest facelift Grand models are only slightly older. As such, with most models still in the comforting care of the franchised dealer network, there isn't too much to worry about – unless it's how to pay for your new purchase. To date, 21st century Jeeps are holding their values well, which is good news if you own one, but a necessary evil if you want to get a foot on the Jeep ladder. To this we have to add the fact that the recent Mercedes connection is not a bad one to have. Teutonic build-quality is legend and when this factor is mixed in to an already well-made vehicle, it's no real surprise to find that the later models have acquired an excellent reputation for hanging together in an impressively reliable manner.

Size matters

Once you've decided to buy American, the next choice is one of size; the Cherokee is much smaller than the Grand version, car-like almost. If you don't need the extra interior space (both for people and luggage) then perhaps the Cherokee is for you. You'll save on purchase price, fuel and other running costs, getting generally better performance and have a car that's easier to park at Sainsbury's on a busy Saturday morning. However, the Grand makes a more impressive statement on the road and can swallow impossible amounts of luggage and people with ease. In terms of off-roading ability, Jeep has had 60 years' practice in making vehicles work in the mud and as the illustrations in Chapter Three show, getting stuck in *any* Jeep takes a lot of effort.

Having decided on size, what about your preferred engine? The six- and eight-cylinder petrol engines are powerful gems, make lovely rumbling noises at rest and glorious howls when extended, but of course, the price you pay is at our over-taxed petrol pumps. As such, the fuel-efficient diesel options are far more popular, the 2.8 CRD especially. The 2.4L petrol engine in the Cherokee is rather lacking in power and torque for a vehicle of this size and capability and is not so popular because of it. For off-roading and/or heavy-duty work, such as towing, it's definitely not the weapon of choice.

In terms of specification, all Cherokees large or small are well-equipped, it's just that some are slightly more well-equipped than others. Leather trim is desirable and will make the car easier to resell, the same principle applying to air conditioning. Add-on goodies such as bull bars and extra lamps etc., can make one car more appealing than the next, but shouldn't affect the price overmuch.

A service history is essential if you're buying a younger car – say four to five years – but after that, it will probably have left the dealer network. More care is required here.

Signs of neglect such as scuffed and cracked bumpers, dents and dings in the bodywork and carpets getting dirty and worn because there's no protective over-mats, all point to less-than-caring owners. Low-mileage isn't the Holy Grail it once was, and very often, a slightly higher-mileage vehicle with a well-stamped service book can be a better buy than one which has yet to be seen by the dealer. If buying from a dealer (either franchised or specialist) a cast-iron warranty is one of the trade-offs for contributing to their end-of-year profit figures. Buying private means you forgo that in exchange for a hefty discount off the dealer price. Checking its provenance (as covered earlier) is extremely important, as modern thieves get better at cloning and ringing stolen and written-off vehicles.

Buying an older Cherokee

The original Cherokee, as introduced to the UK in 1993, retained its basic boxy shape and trademark 'flattened' roof throughout its lifetime until it was replaced by the very different Series 2 car in 2001. The most important major changes occurred in 1997, when it received an exterior facelift which was very subtle, carefully honing the sharp edges of the original. More serious surgery occurred on the inside and out went the 'jukebox' style layout which attracted constant criticism from reviewers, and in came a much more European dash. Although few would argue that it was better from all angles, especially inside, if you don't mind a few extra sharp corners and a dated dash, consider pre '97 cars. These are virtually the same under the skin and can be real bargains. The lowered roof line and generally smaller dimensions did what they were supposed to, in that the Cherokee looked more car-like than the competition. However, it can be a bit awkward for taller drivers and whatever your height, it also lacks a little in terms of elbow room, so try before you buy. There's plenty of luggage space in the rear, despite also having to house the spare tyre,

but rear-seat passengers don't do so well, so if you're regularly going to be carrying a car load around, then make sure it really will do the job.

Grand Cherokee

Having made the case for the smaller car, there's no denying that the Grand is, in fact, a grand car. It is equally well made and, in common with most American vehicles, comes loaded to the gunwales with goodies. It is more or less Series 1 or 2 Range Rover size with a similar on-road presence but is undeniably better-built and finished. In fact, the build-quality is one of the main reasons why it has become popular with disenchanted Land Rover owners. The Grand was introduced into Europe in 1993 at the same time as the Cherokee, but unlike the smaller car, it was a brand-new design, rather than a rehashed 1980s vehicle. However, it wasn't officially available in RHD form until 1996. Again, the first-generation UK cars can appear a bit dated, as they too were very angular and the facelift in 1999 made them look much better.

If you've not driven a large off-roader before, it is as well to have a trial run beforehand – it's an acquired taste with plusses and minuses, and while many love it, some find it too much to handle.

All models

Despite their off-roading abilities, most Jeeps spend their time with all four wheels planted firmly on the

Series 1 Cherokees have leaf springs at the rear which regularly fail as here – check out the height between tyre and bodywork front and rear. If it's noticeably lower at the rear, replacement springs are required.

tarmac. Nevertheless, have a good look round underneath for signs of off-roading damage. They're both large vehicles, so look carefully for signs of bumps and bangs, particularly on the corners – those big plastic bumpers aren't cheap. Doors, too, are vulnerable to parking dings.

Look under the car to check that the engine, gearbox, transfer box and differentials (front and rear) aren't caked in oil, although realistically, older cars will probably show signs of a weep or two. If you view the car where it's usually parked, you'll get a good idea from looking at the area underneath the car for signs of regular overnight oil leakage.

All came with twin fixed roof rails and the cross rails should be included in the car – hack the price accordingly if not. All models rode on alloy wheels, the styles of which varied throughout its life and it's quite acceptable to swap early for late and vice versa. As such, you *can't* tell a model or its year by the wheels. It also means that where wheels have corroded by the elements (very common in the dismal, damp and salt-obsessed UK) changing them shouldn't be too much hassle – buying a second-hand set is quite simple, either privately or from a dismantler. Be more wary of heavily 'kerbed' wheels, which implies an owner who has been rather careless (or who goes rock-crawling at the weekends). In addition, constantly bashing the wheels can damage various other components.

Tyres should be the correct size and all four should be the same make and type – a mix-and-match combination suggests an owner trying to run on a shoestring and should sound warning bells. Look for plenty of tread and for signs of uneven wear, which indicates steering or suspension problems. Bigger tyres than standard look macho but can limit steering lock and will always place extra strain on the front steering and suspension components.

Looking from the side, make sure the car is sitting level. The Cherokee's leaf springs in particular are prone to getting a bit weary, although overworked coil springs (all four corners on the Grand, remember) can sometimes crack. With your torch, peer under the wheelarches for a look at the springs and then the dampers; what you don't want to see are signs of fluid leaking out of them. Don't confuse with the water

which has splashed up from driving however. Overall, replacing springs and dampers isn't that expensive, as there are many specialists around who can offer uprates and alternatives. They do make bargaining points but they should also be seen as part of the whole – if someone is running round with duff suspension, what else awaits?

Using that torch again, try to get a look at the brake pads; all Cherokees are heavier than 'normal' cars and so wear brake pads at an increased rate – the Grand autos are particularly hard on their stoppers. If the pads are wearing unevenly, it might point to a sticking brake calliper. Check the condition of the discs for scoring and correct thickness. You should take a look at the various brake pipes for signs of damage or corrosion and make sure flexible pipes aren't cracked or 'ballooning' where a weak pipe is giving way under braking pressure.

Engines

The 4.0-litre engine is a gem and is virtually bullet-proof unless seriously mistreated. Of course, it's been around forever (which shows in some elements of its design) and it is a big heavy old lump, but nothing is for nothing. It's powerful, smooth and torquey and

There's little but good to say about the six-cylinder, 4.0-litre engine. It's smooth, surprisingly economical and hides no nasty surprises unless it's been mistreated. Problems usually stand out a mile.

mating it to the equally smooth auto box produced a fine combination. It had a few internal modifications in 1996 but was otherwise essentially unchanged. Fuel consumption is surprisingly good, getting to the late teens or even early 20s in general motoring and towards 30mpg on longer, motorway runs. Buy a V8 engine only if you're prepared to spend a lot of time filling that fuel tank – pottering around, you'll be lucky to get to 15mpg. The upside is that unless it's run dry of oil, it will probably outlast the car bodywork by several years.

The four-cylinder petrol engine has never been that popular, not that it is intrinsically bad, just that it struggles a little to cart all that weight around. Other than the usual engine checks, there's little to worry about, except that you might be buying the wrong car.

The four-cylinder VM diesel engine is more economical at the expense of smoothness and sophistication. However, it isn't much-loved in that part of the trade responsible for maintaining and repairing it. One variously hears tales of oil leaks, cracked cylinder heads, inlet and exhaust gaskets blowing, air-conditioning drive links falling off and wrecking the power steering pump, and split turbo intercooler pipes. Another failing on earlier cars was that the ring gears

would shatter which seems to be down to having too fine a pitch on the starter motor. Obviously, these don't affect every single car and many owners are happy with their oil-burners, but there's no smoke (no pun intended!) without fire and great caution is required. Quite honestly, unless you do a mega-mileage, you'll probably not be much worse off financially in the long run by choosing the petrol engine.

Also, the diesel wasn't available with an auto gearbox, which may be a deciding factor for many. A manual box on any large(ish) 4x4 vehicle is seldom as successful as a self-shifter, bearing in mind there's two gearboxes to sort out. The manual 'box is fine as far as it goes, but it's big and cumbersome and by definition, rather clumsy in operation.

The 3.1TD – effectively the 2.5TD with an extra cylinder – is better thought of and being of greater capacity with more power and torque, is more suited to the job in hand. From the end of 1999, it was mated to an auto box in the Grand Cherokee which made life better still.

The 2.5-litre diesel engine, though, isn't so well thought of, there being a long list of faults which have blighted its existence. The five-cylinder version has a much better reputation.

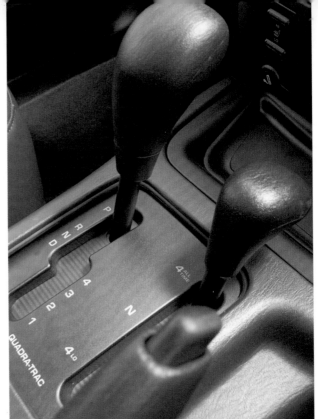

On Series 1 Cherokees, differential bearings can be a problem. Listen for a whining noise. This is the pinion shaft from a 4.0-litre model where the disintegrating bearing was neglected; the cost then became a complete axle – around five times the price of sorting a diff bearing set. Ouch.

Still in the same area, limited slip differentials (4.0 litres up to 1996 and all Series 1 diesels) can go the same way. This is the carrier which holds the clutch plates. The hole for the central pin can also wear. Again, listen for strange whining noises and a juddering which gets progressively worse.

Jeep transmissions are rugged and hard-wearing but should be checked carefully nonetheless. Make sure you try every ratio including those in low-box. Anything that doesn't work perfectly is likely to be expensive to fix.

Check the fluid levels on all engines, oil in particular. Look for signs of water in the oil – a mayonnaise-type sludge when removing the filler cap is an indication – and for oil leaks in the engine bay.

All petrol Cherokees and Grand Cherokees were equipped with a catalyst, so take a look and check its condition. If it looks old and rusty and/or if you can hear it rattling, the odds are it needs expensive replacement. Remember that a failed cat means no MoT certificate. If an MoT test is due, it might be as well to make a purchase dependent on a pass. Other than that, exhausts are fairly conventional and not particularly pricey.

A tow bar suggests, of course, that the car has been used for towing. Both models are quite capable of pulling quite large trailers so be especially picky when it comes to engine and transmission performance, not to mention those rear springs/dampers.

Transmission

Jeep transmissions are as rugged as the image and stand up to plenty of use and abuse. You're unlikely to find too many problems, but that shouldn't stop you looking. Remember that you're dealing with large 4WD vehicles, and the transmission/drivetrains are complicated, involving a gearbox, transfer box, two propshafts, two (or three) differentials, and two axles. The gear selection process is never going to be GTi-slick and if you're not able to differentiate between typical Jeep clonking and something nasty in the works, then take along someone who is. With a manual box, try all the gears and make sure they don't jump out unexpectedly on hard acceleration or deceleration – most likely with first and second. With autos, make sure that in 'D' the car pulls through all the gears and kicks down smartly when required. With all models, make sure you try the low ratios – in some cases, they've not been used since the car was manufactured! You can expect a little more noise than in a family runabout, but excess whining and droning is a cause for concern. There's no doubt that auto boxes work best in Jeeps of any hue and manual cars are generally less desirable.

Air conditioning

Most Jeeps were fitted with air conditioning, later models also having climate control (where the driver could select a specific temperature from a digital readout). Aircon is notoriously expensive when major parts are required, so make sure it works as it should, at very hot as well as very cold. Many owners

switch off the aircon for long periods of time in order to save a few pence on fuel – a bad move! It is far better long term to run aircon as often as possible, ideally all the time. If a system has been unused for too long, it can do more harm than good and if allowed to run 'dry', some of the seals could be damaged.

By definition, all systems lose around 10 per cent of their gas year on year and will need recharging every few years as a matter of course. This in itself should be regarded as part of your maintenance budget, a typical recharge being around £100.

Inside

Having a long list of standard equipment is a Jeep speciality, so don't be bowled over by long descriptions – most Jeeps have air conditioning, electric windows, mirrors and seats etc. As with general build-quality, these goodies are well made and seem to last forever, but you must make sure *everything* works as it should, as replacements can be expensive. Don't be afraid to push every switch and button. Leather seats were fitted to most Jeeps and should be preferred – unless there's a good financial incentive otherwise. The fit and finish of the trim is very good, even on cars ten years old or more, so everything should still click neatly into place.

Use your torch to make sure that the major mechanical bits under the car are not dripping with oil. This engine, gearbox and transfer box are commendably free of exterior oil. A slight weep shouldn't be a worry, but a constant drip certainly should be.

While you're under there, look hard at the suspension; make sure coil springs have no breaks and that the dampers aren't showing signs of leakage.

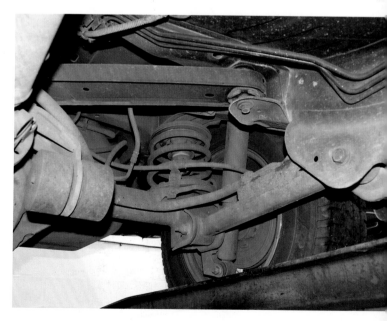

Chapter **Six**

Owning, running and looking after a Cherokee

This section relates specifically to the vehicles available in the UK since 1993.

Unlike a great many modern cars, many UK Jeep models can be serviced and fettled in general by the competent DIY-er. Although it's true that later models – (for example, a fully specified Grand Cherokee) can be an electronic nightmare for the uninitiated, in most other aspects they retain a relative simplicity. The key point is to select what you are capable of doing, and what you are not – messing around with complex electronics can leave you with a non-functioning Jeep and a similarly dysfunctional bank balance to go with it!

Tools and conditions

All Jeeps are large heavy-duty cars which means you need sockets and spanners and other tools of the same ilk – a 3/8in socket set will soon wilt under the pressure. Buy good quality at all times because you will often be applying lots of pressure to the various fasteners and you need to know your ratchet is not going to strip a tooth at a vital moment – taking your knuckles with it.

One of the most common 'tools' you will need is a healthy stock of WD-40 or similar releasing agent. Rust gets just about everywhere and few threads will play the game once a car is a few years old. Make a habit of smearing a dab of copper grease on each fastener you replace – including the wheel nuts and studs; you'll soon come to appreciate the wisdom in doing this, especially if you're changing a flat on the hard shoulder of the M6.

Left: Straddling a deep gully like this makes that suspension work hard. Note deep treaded tyres and the spare already off its mountings in the rear, ready for action. (Nick Dimbleby)

When raising your Jeep for any reason, never forget that it is a considerable weight and will do you a power of no good if it drops on you. Take the matter seriously and use a good quality trolley jack with a large saddle to lift it – a bargain basement, £20 jack isn't something to be recommended – and never work under *any* car when the jack is the only means of support. Use good quality, decent-sized axle stands placed at suitable, solid points and use at least two stands every time. Where possible consider doing the work when all four wheels are on the ground. If this isn't possible, check out any high-torque fasteners and see if you can 'break' them before raising the vehicle. It's forward thinking like this that could save your life.

Below: It's hard to fully service your Jeep without some heavy-duty tools to complement your existing set-up. A ¹/₂in drive socket set and large spanners are a starting point. If you're really serious, go for some ³/₄in drive sockets. (Teng Tools)

Power tools make life much easier and air-tools are probably safer than electric in a garage environment – powered by a compressor you don't have to concern yourself with an electric cable trailing across the workshop (possibly falling into oil or coolant patches) and/or getting snagged or cut on bits of rusty bodywork. There's just about any tool you could care to think of and a few more you wouldn't. Remember to wear eye and ear protection when using pneumatic tools.

Keeping warm is essential if you're to have a clear head and not start rushing the job, especially in the UK where summers are notoriously short. A propane heater may be noisy but it will provide prodigious heat both quickly and cheaply.

Having dirty hands was once the only way to tell a real mechanic, but not any more. Oil has been found to be carcinogenic so keeping your hands clean is important. Wear thin gloves if you can – vinyl and latex are the most common. The nitrile type cost a bit more but they are much more durable. If you can't use gloves (for example, on particularly fiddly work), use a barrier cream on your skin before starting work. When washing your hands, use a decent cleaner which contains moisturiser to prevent them getting painfully chapped.

Keeping warm is vital when you're working on your Jeep – if you start to get too cold, you'll think less clearly, start to make mistakes and find it difficult to do even the simplest things as your fingers go numb. Even a modest propane heater will soon heat up your garage and make life more pleasant – and safer.

Engines

Whether you favour petrol or diesel, and regardless of the number of cylinders, one aspect is paramount – the oil change. If you do a typical average mileage (10–12,000 miles) then an annual oil change is fine. But if you do a much lower mileage, increase your oil change regime accordingly.

Equally important is the need to keep the engines cool. Coolant should be a 50/50 mix of anti-freeze and water, although 'anti-freeze' isn't quite a big enough term nowadays. The stuff on sale today does a dual job of keeping the freezing point lower in the winter and the boiling point higher in the summer. In addition, it keeps the radiator and pipework clean. Diesel engines are noted for their lack of tolerance with regard to overheating and can easily blow a cylinder head gasket and warp the head itself – an expensive occupation.

All petrol-engined Jeeps from 1992 were fitted with catalytic exhausts because of legal requirement. Cats are notoriously expensive to replace and unlike conventional exhaust boxes, don't have to be rotted through to be useless. They're relatively fragile and if you knock one hard enough, it can be wrecked internally – bear this in mind when going off road. However, it is just as easy to damage a cat by knocking it on a kerb. It shouldn't affect the running of the car because the engine management will compensate electronically, and so you probably won't be aware of a problem – until it comes to MoT time, when the emissions will be way too high and a 'fail' is inevitable. Purchasing a replacement will not be a happy occasion, but because so many vehicles are fitted with cats, the aftermarket suppliers can usually offer an alternative make at a considerable saving.

Electrical equipment

Most of the electrical equipment, such as electric windows, sunroof and central locking etc., is fairly conventional stuff. Because Jeeps are made in America, where luxury is always expected to be present, correct and working, electrical faults are comparatively rare. Not unnaturally, replacing, say, an electric seat motor from a franchised dealer isn't cheap, but it is worth checking the club classifieds and specialists (who may have second-hand units in stock), before taking the plunge.

Drivetrain

Gearbox oil changes aren't as important as those for the engine and it is quite enough to follow the manufacturers' recommendations. You can do most good simply by using the 'box properly in day-to-day use, changing gear at the right time and using low-ratio for heavy duty work such as towing large loads and driving off the tarmac. One thing which will soon land you with a large invoice is using part-time 4WD while the vehicle is on a metalled road. You'll get axle 'wind-up' very quickly and if you indulge too often you'll soon be replacing various drivetrain components.

Tyres

Good tyres aren't cheap so regular inspection is worthwhile. Check the pressures at least weekly and adjust for the type of driving – long sessions of high-speed motorway work require higher pressures than playing in the mud. If you live in a rural area, where bad winter weather drastically affects the driving conditions, consider buying a set of deeper-treaded tyres on 'slave wheels' for winter-only use. The author uses road-biased tyres during the summer, on a set of stylish alloy wheels, with a set of AT (all-terrain) tyres on a second set of wheels (also alloys, but bought very cheaply second-hand), from November to March.

If you fancy going off-roading on a regular basis, the same principle applies.

Suspension

Compared with modern, often electronic, suspension systems, all Jeeps are simple in design. This makes them easy to work on and check. A visual check of hydraulic dampers is usually sufficient to see if there are any obvious leaks. If you've recently been driving in the wet and/or mud, give them a good brush down and wipe them clean so that any leaks can be seen. If you do see any, replace immediately and *always* in at least axle pairs – replacing just one damper is a recipe for disaster. Coil springs need occasional checking (more regularly if you do lots of off-roading) for breakages of

Keep an eye on your tyre pressures (always check when tyres are cold) and inspect your wheels regularly for signs of damage. Steel or alloy, it's advisable to fit locking wheel nuts.

Make sure you look hard at the tread for anything likely to create a puncture, and at the sidewalls for any bulges. When you're driving around in such heavy vehicles, tyres take on a much greater importance.

It is worthwhile removing the road wheels occasionally to make sure all is well behind, especially in the dirty winter months and/or if you go off-roading. A blast with a pressure washer is a good idea so you can see if there's anything requiring your attention; check metal and rubber brake pipes, pads for wear, dampers and springs for damage/breaks/leaks and the various rubber bushes for excessive play. Note the copper grease around the studs to prevent the alloy wheel sticking to the steel hub.

the coils. Again, replacement is required in pairs. Leaf springs are hardy devices, more usually simply getting tired and old rather than breaking – again, serious off-roaders should take more care than most. Uprating to six-leaf (rather than the standard four) springs from specialists such as Old Man Emu is a good idea. In general, replacement is quite straightforward, given some hefty tools, a good strong jack/axle stands and no small amount of elbow grease – suspension components are bolted up good and tight, and with a few layers of rust to their name, can be very recalcitrant to leave home!

Bodywork and chassis

Keeping the bodywork clean is a good move; use a quality car shampoo (never washing-up liquid which contains the enemy of paintwork, salt) and rinse off well. It is best to use a wash mitt – a large 'glove' that fits over your hand – and rinse it off after every application of shampoo so you're not reapplying the dirt you've just removed. Use a quality wax on a regular basis and a dedicated cleaner on exterior plastic trim. With gleaming bodywork you have an opportunity to check for any accident damage or signs of corrosion. You will also be investing for the future, because a car that is only washed once a year will not clean up like one treated well, and this of course affects the resale value.

Invest in a pressure washer and keep the muck and crud from building up underneath. This is essential if you go off-roading because garages get annoyed when you wash off half a ton of forest into their jet wash area! Get into all the nooks and crannies, especially during the winter months when road salt will eat through the steel panels and even the chassis, in double-quick time. It pays also to get plenty of anti-corrosion liquids under there, something like Waxoyl or

Those huge alloy wheels and chunky tyres would make a good prize for some lucky thief, so fit locking wheel nuts as a matter of course. Remember to carry the key with you (in case of a puncture), but make sure it's secreted where a thief can't easily find it.

Dinitrol. It's a messy, summer job but pays dividends. Keep a weather eye on the sills and floor panels, particularly the front foot wells which collect everything the front tyres throw back at them and regularly rot through.

Interior

All Cherokees verge on the luxurious and so more time with the vacuum cleaner is required, along with a little polish here and there. Happily, the interior trim is all very good quality and unlikely to give problems. Investing in a set of carpet mats is a good idea, as it protects the much more expensive original carpets and, again, increases the resale value at sale time.

Buying spares

Buying from a main dealer is the best way to ensure you get exactly the right part, albeit at a price. It's cheaper to go to a specialist, although many parts are main dealer only. For some items, ranging from accessories to aftermarket suspension, there is plenty of choice from the 4x4 accessory companies who cater for various models, not just Jeep. However, by definition, the level of expertise there about specific manufacturers isn't as great as at a Jeep specialists, so it pays to do your homework first.

Security

Car theft in the UK remains high and you are well advised to take it seriously. Regardless of what is fitted as standard to your car, don't tempt the thief by leaving valuables in the vehicle. Fit locking wheel nuts as a matter of course – consistent attack-test winners are the McGard Ultra versions. Vehicle tracking is becoming more common and cheaper, with products such as Smartnav combining it with satnav and traffic info. An interior glass film is always worth having, as it means that a brick or hammer won't smash the glass, making the car more secure when left as well as protecting the occupants from traffic light mugging.

Regular checks

To get the most out of your Cherokee, and to keep it in tip-top condition, there are a few jobs you should do on a regular basis. To a great extent, this applies to older cars, many of which have left the franchised dealership servicing regime.

The idea of this section is to tell you what needs regular attention, and what to check to make sure that you are not let down by a problem that could easily

have been avoided. So often, one small item can be overlooked, only for it to develop into a bigger problem which is then often more expensive to fix. Most of the items that need checking regularly can be found under the bonnet – you shouldn't even have to get your hands dirty!

The first and most important regular check is the engine oil level, ideally once a week. Always make sure your pride and joy is parked on level ground when you

Making sure the oil level is correct is about the easiest under-bonnet task there is but it is probably the most important. Letting your engine run low (or out!) means a new engine – compare the cost with that of a few litres of oil every year – no contest.

make the check, and wait at least five minutes after stopping the engine – to allow all the oil to run back into the sump – before you pull out the dipstick. Preferably, check this when the engine is stone cold. If you need to top-up, make sure you use good-quality oil, and don't overfill. Remember, though, that the straight-six engine was designed in a different age and with different tolerances to the modern diesels and later, more hi-tech V8 units. As such, an all-singing synthetic oil is usually unnecessary – as a rule, a good-quality 20w/50 or 10w/40 is fine, and certainly never top up with synthetic if you have mineral oil in the engine. Later engines tend to need a higher grade – your handbook will give exact details.

The brake fluid level should be checked regularly, especially if your Jeep gets a lot of off-road use. It is just possible that if you've been driving over rough terrain you could have damaged a brake hydraulic line – not a problem that you want to discover for the first time as you fail to stop at a busy road junction! It's true that the car has dual-circuit brakes, but the difference in braking ability when one of them is lost is massive.

The coolant level should always be correct but in addition, the ratio of anti-freeze to water should right, too: 50/50 mix is ideal. A tester from your local accessory store costs very little and it could save you from a summer boil-up or a winter freeze.

Brake fluid level will drop very slowly as the brake friction material wears, but you should hardly notice this, and any significant drop in fluid level indicates a leak somewhere in the system. In this case, don't drive the car until the problem has been found and fixed.

While you're under the bonnet, it is wise to also check the coolant level. This is checked in the expansion tank, and should always be done with the engine cold. If you need to top-up, remember that using water is OK on occasions, but if you add only water regularly you are diluting the strength of the coolant, which will reduce its anti-corrosion and anti-freeze properties. Remember that a 50 per cent mix of coolant and water is your aim; you can buy simple and cheap checkers from most DIY stores so you're not leaving this very important maintenance aspect to luck. This means that the freezing-point of the coolant is lowered in winter (typically to –20°C or more) and raised in the summer, to prevent the engine freezing solid or boiling up respectively. It also inhibits corrosion within the water galleries, pump, thermostat etc.

Keep the washer fluid level topped up too – you can guarantee that if you don't, the fluid will run out when you need it most, typically when driving on a salty winter road, or when following a tractor down a muddy lane! Add a reputable screen wash to the water to help clean the screen and to lower the freezing temperature.

Right, nearly there, just two more levels to check, namely power steering fluid and automatic transmission fluid (where applicable). The power steering fluid is checked using a dipstick attached to the reservoir filler cap. The fluid level should be checked with the engine stopped, and the front wheels set in the straight-ahead position. The only reason for the fluid level being low is a leak. A slight weep can go on for years before becoming serious – as long as the level is topped up regularly. To drive a Cherokee without power steering, you will need the physique of a body builder, so it is worth keeping an eye out for leaks! That physique will also come in handy when it comes to lifting the large wads of cash you'll need for replacement parts – a few extra drops of fluid are far cheaper. However, if you're topping up regularly, further investigation is required, not least since a serious leak will cause an MoT failure.

If you have a model with automatic transmission, the fluid level should be checked regularly as recommended in the vehicle handbook or manual. Nine times out of ten, automatic transmission problems are

due to low fluid level. Some care is required as the gearbox oil has to be hot – a drive of around 15 miles is recommended beforehand – and has to be checked with the engine running (handbrake on and transmission in 'park').

That's all the underbonnet checks finished, but there are still just a couple more items that are worth looking at once a week at least. Check your tyre pressures – those large lumps of rubber make it very easy to pick up a slow puncture. Always do this when the tyres are cold, and if possible, use the same gauge every time – different gauges can often give surprisingly different readings. Get your own accurate gauge because forecourt gauges take a lot of mistreatment and are notoriously unreliable. Remember to include the spare, topping that up to 5–10psi more than is required, to allow for any slight deflation before it is needed; you can always let out a few psi, but adding pressure by the side of a busy motorway, in the pouring rain and in pitch black is a bit more tricky!

Finally, the wiper blades; all that's needed here is a quick look to make sure they are not split or damaged.

Check the power steering fluid regularly and top up when required. If the level falls quickly (typically, a noticeable drop within a week) it suggests a serious leak somewhere which should be addressed sooner rather than later to prevent further damage occurring.

It's worth renewing the blades once a year, even if they seem in good condition, as over time they tend to pick up grease from the road which will smear the glass, usually most noticeably when a car is coming towards you at night with the headlights glaring. It pays to give the rubbers a wipe over with a damp cloth to make sure they haven't picked up any tiny sharp stones which could mark the windscreen. It doesn't need too long before it is scratched beyond repair – and even if you're insured you will still have to pay the excess.

And that's it! It should only take ten minutes or so to carry out these checks, but it's time well spent which will help you to pick up on any problems before they develop into anything serious, and you'll have the peace of mind that you shouldn't have any nasty surprises on your next epic journey which could easily have been avoided.

Chapter Seven

It's a Jeep – but not as we know it!

Vehicle manufacturers take every opportunity to present concept cars, the major motoring shows from Tokyo to Geneva being ideal stages to show the way they see their products developing and, just as importantly, to gauge public and professional opinion. We see glimpses of what are currently exotic materials and futuristic engines shown as being commonplace in the next decade or so; some of these windows on the future are quite encouraging, others rather less so, but

over the years, Jeep has produced some gems, a selection of which is featured here.

Jeep Icon

The Jeep Icon concept was shown at the North American International Auto Show in Detroit during January 1997. The company saw it as a vehicle capable of driving America's world-renowned Rubicon Trail off-road course. 'Jeep Icon is a creative exploration for a

Left: The Willys concept showed how designers viewed the future. As with all such vehicles, it's interesting to refer back and see how many features make it to production.

Below: Most concept cars are excessive in every area in the hope that some features will make it to production. This 1997 Icon looks as if it ought to be in production – now!

next-generation Jeep Wrangler,' said John E. Herlitz, Chrysler Corporation's Vice President of Product Design. 'It's solid, stable, built like a rock and its capabilities have been further enhanced.'

Chrysler designers achieved Icon's compact, muscular look by increasing the size of its bumper, tyres and wheelarches. 'Our objective was to give Icon a trim, poised look while keeping much of Jeep Wrangler's unique character,' said Trevor Creed. 'However, we widened the Wrangler's track, reduced its length by 5in, its overhang by 2in, and increased the wheel travel from 8in to 10in.'

Traditional Jeep Wrangler design cues, including its long dash-to-axle proportions, classic grille face, exposed hinges, folding windshield and roll cage were redefined and updated for the next century. 'We wanted to capture the essence of practical product design which fits the Jeep image,' remarked Creed. 'We kept the familiar grille, but made it shorter and wider. We also kept the exposed hinges, bold bumpers, exposed door handles and fuel cap which were designed to give the vehicle more of a mechanical industrial design feel, and at the same time add a lot of intrinsic value. Where the vehicle differs the most is that it is designed as a unibody construction with an integrated aluminium roll cage.'

The show car was painted Steel Blue Metallic, its interior deliberately simple and rugged with the same exposed aluminium fittings and painted steel. One of the Icon's most notable interior design elements was its seats, lightweight and made of exposed aluminium tubes which supported durable waterproofed olive-grey leather upholstery.

Icon designer Robert Lasler said his overall concept was inspired by the design elements found on today's high-end mountain bikes. 'Just like top-of-the-line mountain bikes and our current line-up of Jeep sport utility vehicles, Icon was built to go anywhere,' he said. 'Its parts are high-quality, lightweight and purpose-built. To communicate the quality of each part, we branded our Jeep logo on Icon's hinges, door handles, wheels and bumpers.'

'As we move closer and closer to the next century, Jeep enthusiasts will be happy to know their Jeep will still look like a Jeep,' confirmed Creed.

Jeepster

In January 1998, Chrysler again alluded to the Rubicon Trail, this time suggesting they could build a V8 powered sports car that could just as easily handle this granddaddy of off-road excursions. 'The project began as a Jeep studio designer initiative to create a crossover vehicle,' said Mike Moore, Chrysler's chief designer for the interior and exterior of Jeep products. 'It was a "what if?" exercise. What if you could have the power and excitement of a sports car coupled with the capability and rugged go-anywhere nature of a Jeep Wrangler?'

The basis of the Jeepster was a life-style vehicle that was as competent and fun to drive on fast, twisty black-top roads as it was off-road. The unique, adjustable suspension became an essential feature which enabled this extraordinary capability and the name, originally 'Project Grizzly', was borrowed from the rare 1950 Willys convertible.

The Jeepster's electronic, four-wheel-independent, adjustable suspension raised or lowered the vehicle 4in and adjusted the attitude for a more aerodynamic on-road ride. On-road, the vehicle had a ground clearance of 5¾in, which improved ride and handling by lowering the centre of gravity and better managing the airflow. Off road, the vehicle could be adjusted to a 9¾in ground clearance, necessary for serious rock climbing. The suspension was controlled by two switches on the console.

It had short overhangs (to the joy of serious off-roaders), four-speed automatic, Quadra-Trac II transmission with 4WD high and low-range, and an aluminium skid plate integrated in the side sill. Neat touches included front tow loops integrated into the hinge modules of the forward-hinging hood.

Power was not an issue – the two-plus-two seater came equipped with the all-new 4.7-litre 32-valve V8 engine – the same engine that was to debut on the new 1999 Jeep Grand Cherokee. A dual exhaust system with 3in diameter pipes showed that this sports car meant business.

The body, painted an intense red with contrasting deep blue wing flares and side panels, started with the traditional Jeep grille. Its seven slots were flanked by uniquely detailed headlamps, placed high on the steeply raked grille for lighting efficiency. The front of the hood was lowered to maximise forward visibility, the result being the development of distinctive hood forms tapering back from the headlamps. Design cues were clearly taken from the Plymouth Prowler, with the vehicle sitting lower in the front and higher at the rear to give the appearance of forward motion, even when standing still. The roll cage and soft-top cover worked in the same way as that of the Jeep Icon.

The instrument panel had a look reminiscent of Jeep's military products of the past, while the compact, multi-function heater controls were arranged concentrically in a new style. The navigational system was a reconfigurable coloured flat screen display including a global positioning satellite (GPS) system, altimeter, grade and roll indicator, and an exterior temperature sensor. The cognac seats were made of the same weather-resistant leather as rugged hiking boots.

The front seats were structural and featured a four-point integrated belt system with a centre clasp; the rear seats had conventional three-point belts and folded down for extra cargo room.

The deeply sculpted, five-spoke, 19-inch wheels, with Goodyear extended mobility tyres (EMT), were capable of maintaining their shape, on and off road, even after a puncture, at speeds up to 55mph for distances up to 50 miles. This eliminated the need for a spare, reducing the weight of the vehicle and creating more useful space for luggage. (Goodyear EMT tyres had first appeared on the Plymouth Prowler.)

Jeep Varsity

Shown in early 2000, the Varsity, while appearing initially quite normal for a concept car, was actually an impressive attempt to combine a whole series of design styles. The PR blurb did it better, suggesting that 'the go-anywhere, do-anything, urban adventure concept blurred

The Jeepster was dune buggy-meets-Cherokee, with more than a hint of 32-valve powerful V8.

the line between boulevard and boulder performance'.

The seven-slotted grille and trapezoidal wheel openings mark it out as having Jeep parentage from a distance while the lowered roof-line shouts of first-generation Cherokees.

According to Tom Gale, Executive Vice President Product Development and Design, 'We melded the versatility of a five-door hatchback with a unique roofline and the Grand Cherokee's capability. As sporty and powerful as it is, the Varsity is a true Jeep vehicle. This concept is as adventurous as the people who drive Jeep vehicles today – whether in an urban environment or off-road.'

The Jeep Varsity was powered by a 3.5-litre, 300bhp, 255lb ft V6 engine coupled to a four-speed electronically controlled automatic transmission and a shift-on-the-fly transfer case with full-time four-wheel drive, rear-wheel drive and four-wheel drive low-range modes.

Custom independent front and rear suspension with coil-over-shock set-up and massive 19-inch wheels with P235/55R tyres provided the ride and handling expected from a sports saloon. Estimated performance figures included a sprint to 60mph in 7.1 seconds and a top speed of 130mph.

Not quite sure about the Varsity. The 300bhp engine would certainly appeal, but it seems to lack the instant off-road appeal that should symbolise Jeep.

The sport-utility command-of-the-road seating positions combined with robust bumpers, substantial wheel flares and side sill, a strong character line and high belt made the Varsity a heavy-duty car.

There was even a high level of confidence in the alloy wheels, a five-spoke design executed with faceted aluminium billets, not a million miles away from the latest Grand Cherokees. Head and tail lamps echoed the Jeep heritage and gave improved light output to enhance the vehicle's safety and security.

Together with the vehicle's athletic stance, the rear design showed off the Varsity's tailored sporty personality. Impressive centre-mounted chrome double exhaust pipes, its round lamp treatment and the oversized Jeep name on the deck lid shouted performance. Chiselled lines in the bumper, deck lid and lamp surrounds made for a powerful design statement. Overall, this generated an all-new rear 'face' for a Jeep vehicle.

The interior mimicked the exterior design with substantial shapes, strong lines and a backbone-style centre console running through the vehicle. The symmetrical instrument panel incorporated large round gauges with tipped-out angular surfaces and yellow-green glowing back lights. Executed in heavy duty materials, the interior was meant to suggest a seriously rugged, off-road-type vehicle; the sort you'd use for a day out cutting down redwoods, that kind of thing.

Jeep Willys Concept

The Willys, unveiled at the 2001 North American International Auto Show in Detroit, featured plastic body technology, allowing for a radical approach to Jeep design while remaining true to the brand's legendary capability. The back-to-basics, composite-bodied Jeep Willys concept vehicle paid homage to Jeep vehicles of the past while showcasing the design and technology of the 21st century.

'We designed this concept vehicle with the self-expressive, free-thinker in mind,' said Trevor Creed, Senior Vice President – Product Design, DaimlerChrysler Corporation. 'The Jeep Willys' usefulness and versatility were developed to exist in ecological harmony with nature while being perfectly suited for the rigors of an active lifestyle. Call it the pure American.'

Much was made of the injection-moulded plastic bodies, which saved up to 50 per cent in weight and manufacturing costs and were nearly 100 per cent recyclable. The moulded-in-colour plastic allowed designers to create shapes not permitted with stamped

metal, such as the crisp, rigid lines that gave the Willys its high-tech, machined appearance.

The Jeep Willys's frame-web technology moulded the one-piece carbon fibre body to a lightweight aluminium frame, giving it industry-leading rigidity.

As ever, the seven-slot grille led the way and those wheelarches looked vaguely familiar. The short rear overhang gave it an athletic stance as well as being good news for more serious off-roaders.

'My "pure American" design philosophy for the Jeep Willys led me to the very clean, precise and mechanical appearance,' said Jordan Meadows, Product Designer at DaimlerChrysler's Pacifica Design Centre in Carlsbad, California. 'However, it still shows traditional Jeep design cues, such as the trademark grille and wheelarches and its commanding feel on the road, as well as off the beaten path.'

This visual character was carried on in the spacious interior which sported a light palette in colours and

Now that's more like it! The Willys Concept looks like it means business with lots of the current Wrangler design cues in its semi open-top layout.

materials. Featured were brushed aluminium and aqua/grey leather with Starbrite Silver accents and, for the techno heads, digital radio was standard.

'In detailing Willys's interior with an honest look and feel, we reinforced the versatile Jeep lineage,' said Meadows. 'The Jeep Willys is a prime example of a vehicle embracing its past while looking to its future.'

Under the bonnet was housed a 1.6-litre, in-line four-cylinder engine, supercharged to deliver 160hp and 155lb ft of torque. Its four-speed automatic transmission was coupled with a shift-on-the-fly transfer case with full-time four-wheel drive and low-range modes. Custom, independent short-and-long-arm front and multi-link solid rear axle suspension with coil-over-shock set-up and sizeable 22-inch

The interior managed to be 21st century upmarket, with lots of aluminium in evidence, while being ready to hose-out after a weekend on the trail. Even the holey seats could be washed in situ.

wheels with P235/840R560 PAX tyres embraced the 'go anywhere' attitude synonymous with the Jeep brand.

Estimated performance figures included 0–60 mph in 10.2 seconds and a top speed of almost 90mph. 'The custom suspension and supercharged powertrain were engineered to preserve the rugged capabilities that the Jeep brand is known for,' added Creed. 'We wanted the DNA of the Willys to speak to the heritage of its ancestors. We were looking for the most efficient yet stylish way to capture the spirit of classic Jeep vehicles enhanced with modern technology. Marrying 21st century technology with 20th century tradition, the pure American Willys captures the bare essence of the Jeep brand.'

It is only natural that the Jeep team thought highly of their baby, but others did, too, as the Willys Concept won the Gold Award in the 2001 Industrial Design Excellence Competition sponsored by *Business Week* magazine and the Industrial Design Society of America.

Jeep Willys2 Concept

Not surprisingly, the Willys2 Concept followed on smartly from its eponymous predecessor. 'Willys2 embodies the Jeep brand's core values of fun, freedom and legendary capability, generating interest from the

young and young at heart,' said Jordan Meadows, a product designer at the Pacifica Advanced Design Centre.

As well as the usual design cues, Willys2 sported a high-tech machined appearance and featured a one-piece carbon fibre body on an aluminium frame and with a removable carbon fibre hard-top. The latter came equipped with a roof rack featuring a full-size spare tyre holder and an integrated luggage carrier, as well as bindings for various kinds of outdoor gear. Three auxiliary fog and search lamps emphasised the 'go-anywhere do-anything' attitude that is characteristic of the Jeep brand.

It featured a custom, independent short-and-long-arm front and multi-link solid rear axle suspension, with coil springs at all four wheels. Inside, the spacious interior was a Tonka-toy mix of tough translucent plastics which retained practicality because, according to Meadows, 'You can still take a water hose to this interior and clean it out,' said Meadows.

Powered by a 160bhp, 1.6-litre, four-cylinder engine, the Willys2 could lug its 1,350kg (3,000lb) weight to 62mph in less than 10 seconds with a top speed of around 90mph.

Jeep Compass Concept

The Jeep Compass, made its world premiere in January 2002 at the North American International Auto Show in Detroit. Jeep's description was that of 'a concept that feels at home in an urban environment while possessing the free spirit of a performance rally car.'

Built on the platform of a Jeep Liberty (Cherokee from 2001 in UK), the Compass offered a great combination of on-road dynamics and off-highway capability. The vehicle was aimed at 'millennials' – the next large emerging group of consumers, now aged 24 or younger. (This group will soon outnumber the 'Baby Boomer' generation.) 'Millennials are looking for an authentic, affordable vehicle to carry their friends and gear,' said Trevor Creed, Senior Vice President of Design for the Chrysler Group. They would prefer to have an exotic sports car, but those are not only out of their financial reach, but also don't offer enough room or flexibility. As such, the Compass was created as a capable compact SUV offering performance, cargo space and an attractive price.

Like a rally car, the two-door Jeep Compass had all-wheel drive, a short wheelbase and a low centre of

Right: The Willys2 went even further, sticking a roof on top and ... lots of outdoor gear on top of that.

No-one could argue that this baby had lots of presence, especially from the rear. Did anyone say 'Hummer'?

gravity to hug the road. It featured a lightweight steel 'uniframe' construction and a 3.7-litre PowerTech V6 engine giving 210bhp/235 lb ft of torque, so whether on or off road, running out of power wouldn't appear to be likely.

The instrument panel looked like the cockpit of a jet fighter with technical dials and gauges while the interior styling was kept simple, uncluttered and functional. Slot machine-style rotating controls operated all primary functions, while the gauges were reminiscent of traditional watch faces.

A sturdy grab handle covered the width of the instrument panel, as a visually strong 'backbone' ran throughout the entire interior. This design element was mirrored by a full-length overhead console. The instrument panel featured a multi-functional docking station with LCD screen. Four bucket seats offered all occupants a command-of-the-road seating position, comfort and support. In the rear, the seats folded forward to create a flat loading surface executed in

low-gloss stainless steel with integrated tie-downs in the side trim. Up top, the roof featured a unique, diamond-plate textured liner with integrated tie-downs, developed to take the abuse of any type of hauling.

The avowed aim of this car was '… to make the Jeep Compass rugged, durable and able to take a beating at all the typical scuff zones'.

Jeep Treo

The Jeep Treo debuted at the 37th Tokyo Motor Show in October 2003 (Tokyo obviously being a favourite for Jeep's off-the-wall department). It's designers aimed to 'look into the future to create an Earth-friendly urban mobility vehicle.'

Clearly aimed at young consumers, it retained, of course, the seven-bar grille and prominent windshield presence, while inside providing space for three passengers or 'two-plus-gear' in a cabin that created an open feel in what was a compact vehicle.

Underneath, the Treo was based on an all-new platform designed to utilise drive-by-wire technology and a zero-emission fuel cell – or other advanced power plant of the future – along with an electric drive powertrain that gave the Treo full-time four-wheel-drive capability.

Its designers were challenged to look a decade or more into the future and extend the Jeep brand's customer base. The result was an urban mobility vehicle that provided Jeep style and freedom in a clean, compact package – one that could adapt to youthful lifestyle demands, both in an urban environment and at the trailhead.

'The Treo is a vivid new interpretation of where the Jeep brand could go in the future using the freedom of fuel cell technology. It truly exemplifies the idea of "fluid imagination" thinking in a stunning, unexpected package,' said Trevor Creed, Chrysler Group's Senior Vice President of Design.

The Treo's front end presented a bold new Jeep signature and provided fresh insights on the classic Jeep 'face'. The vehicle tapered front-to-back in a tear-drop shape, ending with two high-mounted spar wings that housed rear lamps and served as mounts for twin

Bottom right: Somehow the design team has managed to give what is essentially a large, chunky off-roader, the overall look of a sports coupé. Setting the wheel into the rear bumper is a neat touch.

This is the Treo, the car for which the word 'wacky' was made! Ideal for the first off-roader on the moon, or, as it was intended, a 4WD city car. What about those wings with built-in indicators – anyone remember the old days of semaphore indicators?

high-tech Jeep Rubicon mountain bikes – the perfect equipment for tomorrow's active young consumers. The rear hatch with a large cut-out notch gave easy access to rear storage.

But this was no limp-wristed design exercise, the innate ruggedness being signalled by the flared wheelarches that gave the over-sized tyres plenty of play, tow hooks exposed on the front end, and the 'precision tool' look of the headlamps and mirrors. The military-style tyre tread, exposed front suspension and the hiking boot tread detail on the sill plate all enhanced the vehicle's adventurous image.

Of particular interest in terms of manufacturing flexibility were its interior features. The steering wheel and column, pedals, speedometer and other instruments were housed in a single, sculpted module. The entire module slid through a slot in the dash for quick adaptation to right or left-hand driving, extending the Treo's reach to world markets.

The radio, GPS locator and climate controls with touch-screen operation were housed in a second, removable module.

Lightweight seats were made of translucent material over a strong carbon fibre frame. The rear seat folded flat for storage of additional gear. Another configuration allowed for the front wheels from the Rubicon bikes to be removed and mounted in the rear of the interior, while still permitting a third passenger to ride along.

Despite the vehicle's compactness, a feeling of openness was maintained in the interior by the large windshield, a 'see-through', seven-slotted Jeep front grille, and a glass roof that extended over the rear passenger space.

The vehicle was powered by two electric motors driving the front and rear wheels, giving full-time four-wheel drive capability. For the future, the Treo was designed to adapt to new technologies, such as drive-by-wire, fuel cells or other advanced powertrains.

'Treo's visionary vehicle packaging with its basic three-seat configuration and built-in versatility lends itself to future Jeep activity seekers – at entry-level price positioning. It is rugged and functional in genuine Jeep fashion, but its adaptability is taken to the next level,' Creed said.

Appendix A

Specifications

Jeep Cherokee XJ (1993–2001)

ENGINES

Petrol	Capacity (cc)	Bore x stroke (mm)	Power bhp @ rpm	Torque lb ft @ rpm	Comp ratio
4.0 Limited	3,960	98.45 x 86.69	184 @ 4,750	214 @ 3,950	8.75:1
4.0 Limited*	3,960	98.45 x 86.69	181 @ 4,750	221 @ 3,000	8.75:1
2.5L Sport	2,464	98.45 x 80.98	122 @ 5,300	148 @ 3,200	9.13:1

Diesel					
2.5L TD	2,499	92.0 x 94.0	116 @ 4,000	207@2,000	22.0:1

At launch, the Cherokee was available with a choice of four-cylinder, indirect injection diesel and six-cylinder petrol engines, both of which were cast iron, OHV units with multi-point sequential fuel injection. A 36-month/60,000-mile mechanical warranty was included along with a 72-month anti-perforation warranty with recovery service for 12 months. Service intervals were oil change at 7,500 miles and a major at 15,000 miles.

The 2.5-litre VM turbo diesel engine arrived in the UK in early 1995. It was an in-line, four-cylinder unit with cast-iron block and light alloy cylinder heads.

*This engine was slightly modified for the 1996 model year and although power was slightly down, the all-important torque figure rose and, better still, the maximum torque was produced almost 1,000 rpm down the tachometer.

BODY
Uniframe design with extensive use of galvanised steel.

TRANSMISSION
The diesel and 2.5L petrol engines came equipped with a five-speed manual gearbox and the 4.0L petrol, a four-speed automatic, with torque converter lock-up. All were 4WD, the smaller engined cars having the Command-Trac, part-time system (normally 2wd with 4WD having to be selected), while the 4.0-litre models featured Selec-Trac, where full-time 4WD was available with optional 2WD or part-time 4WD (i.e. locked differential).

STEERING
A recirculating ball system with power assistance and hydraulic steering damper, 3.4 turns lock-to-lock.

BRAKES, WHEELS AND TYRES
At the front, 11in (280mm) ventilated discs were fitted along with 10in (254mm) drums at the rear. All models had power brake assistance via a single diaphragm, vacuum-operated brake booster. Anti-lock braking (ABS) was standard on 4.0-litre petrol versions. All rolled on 15in diameter alloy wheels fitted with Goodyear P225/70 R 15 tyres.

SUSPENSION
At the front, there was a Quadra-Link solid axle with four locating arms, heavy duty coil springs, stabiliser bar, steering damper and heavy-duty gas-charged shock absorbers – with anti-roll bar. At the rear were heavy-duty multi-leaf springs, stabiliser bar and heavy-duty gas-charged shock absorbers

DIMENSIONS

Length	4,240mm
Width	1,790mm
Height	1,623mm
Wheelbase	2,576mm
Track (F/R)	1,473/1,473mm
Min. ground clearance (axle)	216mm
Min. running ground clearance	246mm
Turning diameter	11.7m
Headroom (front)	973mm
Headroom (rear)	965mm
Leg room (front)	1,041mm
Leg room (rear)	897mm
Luggage capacity, seat upright	1,011 litres
Luggage capacity, seat folded	2,033 litres
Fuel tank capacity	16.7gall (76 litres)

FUEL CONSUMPTION (MPG)

	2.5L TD	2.5 Sport	Petrol
Urban	28.8	19.5	15.7
Constant 56mph	39.8	28.5	27.4
Constant 75mph	26.9	20.5	19.6

WEIGHTS

	2.5L TD	2.5 Sport	Petrol
Kerb weight (kg)	1,490	1,450	1,535
Max towing weight (kg)	2,500	3,300	3,300

Jeep Cherokee KJ (2001–onward)

ENGINES

Petrol	Capacity	Bore x stroke	Power bhp	Torque lb ft	Comp
	(cc)	(mm)	@ rpm	@ rpm	ratio
2.4L 16v	2,429	87.5 x 101.0	145 @ 5,200	159 @ 4,000	9.5:1
3.7L V6	3,700	93.0 X 90.8	201 @ 5,200	230 @ 3,800	9.9:1
Diesel					
2.5 CRD	2,499	92.0 x 94.0	141 @ 4,000	251 @ 2,000	17.5:1
2.8 CRD	2,776	94.0 x 100.00	148 @ 3,800	266 @ 1,800	17.5:1

The new 'round' Cherokee was blessed with a brand-new line-up of three engines. At the base was a 2.4-litre, four-cylinder, DOHC 16-valve petrol engine. It featured sequential multi-point fuel injection. Popular in the UK was the VM-sourced 2.5-litre, four-cylinder, DOHC, CRD (common rail) turbo diesel unit with a cast-iron block and one-piece cylinder head. At the top of the tree, a 3.7-litre V6 PowerTech petrol engine replaced the venerable, straight-six, four-litre engine. An addition to the line-up at the end of 2002 was the DaimlerChrysler 2.8-litre CRD diesel engine, giving more power, torque and performance.

TRANSMISSION
The 2.4L petrol and 2.5 CRD models featured part-time Command-Trac 4WD with 'shift-on-the-fly' and low-range. They were only available with a five-speed, manual gearbox.

The 3.7L V6 and 2.8 CRD models had full-time Selec-Trac 4WD with 'shift-on-the-fly' and low-range. They were only available with an auto gearbox, four-speed for the diesel and five-speed on the petrol option.

DIMENSIONS

Length	4,496mm
Width	1,819mm
Height	1,817mm
Wheelbase	2,649mm
Track (F/R)	1,524/1,524mm
Turning diameter	10.94m
Luggage capacity, rear seat folded	1,954 litres
Luggage capacity, rear seat upright	821 litres
Fuel tank capacity	19gall (72 litres)

FUEL CONSUMPTION (MPG)

	2.4 petrol	2.5 CRD	2.8 CRD	3.7 V6
Combined	26.9	31.4	28.5	21.7
Extra urban	32.1	37.7	34.4	27.4
Urban	20.2	24.1	22.2	15.2
Emissions CO_2gkm	255	250	262	318

WEIGHTS

	2.4 petrol	2.5 CRD	2.8 CRD	3.7 V6
Kerb weight (kg)	1,891	2,161	2,140	2,056
Max towing weight (kg)	2,400	2,688	3,360	3,360

Jeep Grand Cherokee ZJ (1993–1999)

ENGINES

Petrol	Capacity	Bore x stroke	Power bhp	Torque lb ft	Comp
	(cc)	(mm)	@ rpm	@ rpm	ratio
4.0L	3,960	98.4 x 87.0	174 @ 4,600	222 @ 2,400	8.75:1
5.2L V8	5,216	99.34 x 84.12	212 @ 4,750	285 @ 4,750	9.1:1
5.9L V8	5,899	102 x 91	237 @ 4,050	348 @ 3,050	8.7:1
Diesel					
2.5L TD	2,499	92 x 94	114@ 3,900	205 @ 1,800	20.95:1

Although first produced for the 1993 model year, the Grand Cherokee did not arrive in RHD format until February 1996, when it was available as a 4.0-litre Limited version. The engine was slightly modified from this point and produced rather less power than previously, but with more torque which was lower down the rev range. Multi-point fuel-injection was retained. The first diesel-powered Grand appeared in 1997, the unit being the 2.5-litre, four-cylinder unit which first appeared in the Cherokee Sport that had a cast-iron block and alloy cylinder head and with indirect multi-point fuel-injection. The 5.2-litre V8 was first available in 1994 to special order and in LHD only, as was the 5.9-litre, Limited LX version in 1997.

BODY
A uniframe chassis design with extensive use of galvanised steel.

TRANSMISSION
The 4.0-litre Limited and 5.2L V8 Limited came with four-speed automatic transmission as standard. The 4WD system was the Quadra-Trac permanent four-wheel drive with viscous coupling and limited slip rear differential. The four-cylinder diesel engined cars had a five-speed manual gearbox with Command-Trac part-time 4WD and limited slip rear differential.

STEERING
A recirculating ball system with power assistance, which was speed-sensitive on the petrol-engined cars.

BRAKES, WHEELS AND TYRES
Discs were used all-round, ventilated 11in (279.6mm) at the front and solid, 11.25in (285mm) at the rear. Three-channel, four-wheel-sensor ABS was fitted. The 5.2L Limited, had ventilated 11.2in (284mm) front discs at the front but 10in (250mm) drums at the rear, with discs available as an option. The Limited petrol version had 16 x 7J alloy wheels shod with 225/70R dual-purpose road tyres, whereas the diesel and Laredo petrol-engined cars had 15 x 7J alloys, fitted with Goodyear Wrangler AT 215/75 R15 tyres.

SUSPENSION
At front and rear were rigid axles with four longitudinal links, coil springs, heavy-duty gas-filled shock absorbers and anti-roll bars.

DIMENSIONS
Length	4,500mm
Width/incl. mirrors	1,800/2,081mm
Height	1,752mm
Wheelbase	2,690mm
Track (F/R)	1,473/1,473mm
Turning diameter	11.4m
Luggage capacity, seat folded	2,254 litres
Luggage capacity, seat upright	1,136 litres
Fuel tank capacity	19.2gall (87.4 litres)

WEIGHTS
Kerb weight (kg)	1,820 (diesel 1,835)
Max towing weight (kg)	3,500 (diesel 2,360)

FUEL CONSUMPTION (MPG)
	Diesel	4.0L petrol
Urban	23.0	13.0
Extra urban	36.0	23.5
Combined cycle	29.7	18.2

	Petrol 5.2L V8
Urban	13.9
Constant 56mph	25.7
Constant 75mph	18.6

Jeep Grand Cherokee WJ (1999–onward)

ENGINES

Petrol	Capacity (cc)	Bore x stroke (mm)	Power bhp @ rpm	Torque lb ft @ rpm	Comp ratio
4.0L	3,956	98.4 x 86.7	188 @ 5,000	218 @ 3,050	8.8:1
4.7L V8	4,701	93.0 x 86.5	217 @ 4,700	288 @ 3,200	9.3:1
4.7L V8 HO	4,701	93.0 x 86.5	255 @ 5,200	309 @ 4,000	9.7:1
Diesel					
3.1 TD	3,125	92 x 94	138 @ 3,600	283 @ 1,800	21.0:1
2.7 CRD	2,685	88 x 88.4	161 @ 4,000	295 @ 1,800	18.0:1

From March 1999, the facelifted Series 2 Grand Cherokee was on sale in
the UK. The 4L, straight-six engine was still available, albeit with
modifications and the range was augmented by the addition of the SOHC
4.7L V8 PowerTech engine. Both featured sequential multi-point fuel-
injection. The five-cylinder, 3.1-litre diesel engine arrived in November 1999
and was replaced by the five-cylinder, DaimlerChrysler 2.7 CRD I
powerplant in 2002.

BODY
As previously.

TRANSMISSION
Four-speed auto gearbox with Quadra Trac II permanent four wheel drive
with progressive differential. A five-speed auto was introduced and
available on all models except the 4.0L petrol.

STEERING
A recirculating ball system with power assistance; 2.94 turns lock-to-lock.

BRAKES, WHEELS AND TYRES
Ventilated discs were fitted at the front, with solid discs at the rear. ABS
anti-lock braking was standard. Wheels were 16 x 7J alloys shod with
245/70 R16 tyres and a full-size spare wheel/tyre. Later the wheel and tyre
sizes increased to 17 x 7J with 235/65 HR 17 tyres.

SUSPENSION
Live axle, Quadra link leading arms, track bars, coil springs, anti-roll bar
and gas-charged shock absorbers were used at the front. At the rear it was
a live axle, lower trailing arms, triangular upper arms, coil springs, anti-roll
bar and gas-charged shock absorbers.

DIMENSIONS
Length	4,610mm
Width/incl. mirrors	1,839/2,239mm
Height	1,806mm
Wheelbase	2,691mm
Track (F/R)	1,511/1,511mm
Turning diameter:	11.1m
Luggage capacity, seat folded	2,047 litres
Luggage capacity, seat upright	1,104 litres
Fuel tank capacity	17.2gall (78 litres)
	Later 20.5gall (93 litre)

WEIGHTS
	4.0 Ltd	3.1TD	2.7CRD	4.7 V8	4.7 V8 HO
Kerb weight max (kg)	2,045	1,835	2,135	2,073	2,074
Max towing weight (kg)	3,500	3,500	3,500	3,500	3,500

PETROL ENGINES
Economy (mpg)	4.0 Limited	4.7 V8	4.7 V8 HO
Combined cycle	18.2	17.7	17.8
Extra urban	24.6	22.6	23.5
Urban mpg	12.8	12.8	12.8

DIESEL ENGINES
Economy (mpg)	3.1 TD	2.7 CRD
Combined cycle	24.1	29.1
Extra urban	29.1	34.9
Urban mpg	19.5	22.6

Jeep Wrangler YJ (1993–1995)

(Note – 1993 was the first year of RHD production for the UK, although the
YJ Wrangler had actually been in LHD production since 1986.)

ENGINES

Petrol	Capacity (cc)	Bore x stroke (mm)	Power bhp @ rpm	Torque lb ft @ rpm	Comp ratio
2.5-litre	2,464	98.45 x 80.98	122 @ 5,300	148 @ 3,200	9.13:1
4.0-litre	3,960	98.45 x 86.69	184 @ 4,750	214 @ 3,950	8.75:1

At UK launch, the Wrangler was available with a choice of two petrol engines – the 2.5-litre and 4.0-litre units, which were also available in the Cherokee and were fuelled by the same sequential multi-point injection. Catalytic converters were standard on both engines, requiring the use of unleaded petrol. Both models were covered by a 36-months/60,000-mile mechanical warranty and 72 months anti-perforation cover with recovery service for 12 months. Extra cost options were unlimited mileage and additional 12 months cover/no mileage limit. Service intervals were 7,500 miles oil change/15,000 miles major service.

BODY

This was an all-steel construction with extensive use of galvanised steel (all major panels were heavy-gauge steel which was reinforced, flanged and welded). There was a separate lightweight, rectangular shaped tubular frame chassis, insulated from the body by spacers.

TRANSMISSION

Both engine variants drove through a five-speed manual gearbox. The 4WD system was part-time Command-Trac, with low range. The standard Trac-Lok limited slip rear differential (60 per cent locking) meant that forward progress was still possible even if one of the rear wheels had lost all contact with the ground.

STEERING

A variable-ratio recirculating ball system with power assistance and hydraulic steering damper, taking 3.4 turns lock-to-lock.

BRAKES, WHEELS AND TYRES

At the front, 11in (280mm) ventilated discs were fitted, with 10in (254mm) drums at the rear. Power brake assistance was provided by a single diaphragm, vacuum-operated brake booster. Steel rims were standard on the 2.5L and 4.0L with the 4L Limited model riding on cross-spoke alloy wheels. Standard on both vehicles were Goodyear Wrangler AT (all-terrain) tyres, P215/75R 15.

SUSPENSION

Hotchkiss-type multi leaf springs with dual-action shock absorbers were fitted at both ends of the car, the front also featuring a stabiliser bar.

DIMENSIONS

Length	3,879mm
Width	1,676mm
Height (soft-top)	1,829mm
Height (hard-top)	1,767mm
Wheelbase	2,373mm
Track (F/R)	1,473/1,473mm
Min. ground clearance, axle	206mm
Min. running ground clearance	246mm
Turning diameter	10.6m
Headroom (front driver)	1,021mm
	(soft-top: 1,052mm)
Headroom (front passenger)	1,017mm
	(soft-top: 1,041mm)
Leg room (front driver)	1,001mm
Leg room (front passenger)	991mm
Luggage capacity, rear seat folded	1,223 litres
Luggage capacity, rear seat upright	354 litres
Luggage capacity, rear seat removed	1,512 litres
Fuel tank capacity	16.7gall (76 litres)

FUEL CONSUMPTION (MPG)

	2.5L	4.0L
Urban	20.0	15.8
Constant 56mph	26.9	25.9
Constant 75mph	18.0	17.4

WEIGHTS

	2.5L	4.0L
Kerb weight (kg)	1,395	1,455
Max towing weight (kg)	1,000	1,000

Jeep Wrangler TJ (1996–onward)

ENGINES

Petrol	Capacity (cc)	Bore x stroke (mm)	Power bhp @ rpm	Torque lb ft @ rpm	Comp ratio
2.5-litre	2,464	98.45 x 80.98	117 @ 5,200	138 @ 3,600	9.13:1
4.0-litre	3,960	98.45 x 86.69	174 @ 4,600	214 @ 3,600	8.75:1

The same two engine sizes were available in the revised Wrangler, though the smaller, 2.5 litre option was deleted in 2001.

BODY

The body style and construction followed the previous model although many subtle differences were made, not least due to safety constraints.

TRANSMISSION

A five-speed manual gearbox was standard with an auto option on 4.0L models (the Sahara was auto-only). The 4WD system was part-time Command-Trac, with low range. The standard Trac-Lok limited slip rear differential was fitted.

STEEERING

A recirculating ball and worm system with hydraulic power assistance; 3.0 turns lock-to-lock.

BRAKES, WHEELS AND TYRES

At the front, 11in (280mm) vented discs were fitted with a conventional 9in (229mm) drums at the rear, the wheels being 15-inch x 7J steel or alloy depending on the model. Steel wheels were fitted with 215/75 R15 tyres and the alloys were fitted with 225/75 R15 tyres.

SUSPENSION

Live solid axles were retained with front and rear upper and lower control arms, with stabiliser bars. The major change was that the old-fashioned leaf springs were replaced by coil springs and heavy-duty gas-filled dampers.

DIMENSIONS

Length	3,860mm
Width	1,694mm
Height	1,782mm
Wheelbase	2,372mm
Track (F/R)	1,473mm
Turning diameter	10.25m
Headroom	1,038mm (soft-top: 1,075mm)
Leg room	1,044mm
Luggage capacity, rear seat folded	1,011 litres (soft-top: 1,045 litres)
Luggage capacity, rear seat upright	309 litres (soft-top: 320 litres)
Luggage capacity, rear seat removed	1,515 litres (soft-top: 1,577 litres)
Fuel tank capacity	19gall (72 litres)

FUEL CONSUMPTION (MPG)

	4.0L	4.0L auto
Combined cycle	22.1	20.2
Extra urban cycle	32.1	28.5
Urban cycle	14.4	13.5

WEIGHTS

	2.5L	4.0L
Kerb weight (kg)	1,505	1,570
Max towing weight (kg)	1,125	1,800

Imperial/metric conversions

Car manufacturers and aftermarket suppliers regularly mix and match terminology which, combined with the UK's gradual conversion from imperial to metric make it increasingly tricky for the Cherokee owner to get a total grip on what's what. This simple conversion table will help to ensure that you get it right every time.

To convert	To	Multiply by
Length		
inches	millimetres	25.4
millimetres	inches	0.0394
miles	kilometres	1.609
kilometres	miles	0.6214
Volume		
cubic inches	cubic centimetres	16.387
cubic centimetres	cubic inches	0.061
Imperial gallons	litres	4.546
litres	Imperial gallons	0.22
Weight		
pounds	kilograms	0.454
kilograms	pounds	2.205
Speed		
mph	km/h	1.609
km/h	mph	0.6214
Fuel consumption		
Imperial mpg	kilometres per litre	0.354
	litres-per-100km	divide 283 x gall
kilometres per litre	Imperial mpg	2.825

Bolt identification, metric/imperial and thread

When it comes to sorting out bolt identification, look for an 'S' or an 'R' stamped into the head, which denotes that it is imperial.

Imperial threads-per-inch (tpi)

	4BA	2BA	No. 10	1/4in	5/16in	3/8in	7/16in
BA	38.5	31.4					
UNC			24	20	18	16	14
UNF			32	28	24	24	20
BSF				26	22	20	18
BSW				20	18	16	14

The figure 8.8 in the head shows that it is a metric bolt. The threads on imperial fasteners are shown as threads per inch (TPI). On metric bolts, the pitch is the length of ten threads. So a bolt described as M10 x 1.5 pitch, is one with a shank diameter of 10mm where ten threads cover a distance of 1.5cm. This table shows the pitches used on most* metric bolts

Bolt size	Pitch (mm)
M5	0.8
M6	1.00
M8	1.25
M10	1.5
M12	1.75

* For some reason, the pitch on Japanese 10mm bolts is a finer 1.25 rather than the usual 1.5.

Numerology and sales figures

Identification letters

Once you get involved with the world of Jeeps, you'll find that everyone talks in a two-letter shorthand. For UK reference, here's what you need to know:

YJ – Wrangler (1987–96)
TJ – Wrangler (1997–onward)
XJ – Cherokee (UK) (1993–2001)
KJ – Cherokee/Liberty (2001–onward)
ZJ – Grand Cherokee (1993–1999)
WJ – Grand Cherokee (1999–onward)

UK sales figures up to and including 2003

Year	Cherokee	Grand Cherokee	Wrangler	Total
1993	3,411	0	498	3,909
1994	4,469	46	422	4,937
1995	5,514	56	309	5,879
1996	5,368	4,025	110	9,503
1997	3,951	4,797	840	9,588
1998	4,016	3,762	734	8,512
1999	2,294	4,292	424	7,010
2000	1,984	4,447	374	6,805
2001	2,082	4,534	320	6,936
2002	3,990	4,447	200	8,637
2003	3,932	3,998	199	8,129
Total	37,079	34,404	4,430	79,845

Launch year – 1993 – saw 3,411 Cherokees sold. In 1994, the figure rose to 4,469 and in 1995 it was 5,514. With the arrival in 1996 of the eagerly awaited (RHD) Grand Cherokee, it was inevitable that some previous Cherokee customers would trade up to the Cherokee's bigger stablemate – but Cherokee sales still remained strong. In fact, Cherokee sales in 1996 were 5,368 with Grand Cherokee achieving 4,025. It is interesting to note that over the 10-year period, sales of the Grand Cherokee are almost equal to those of its smaller sibling, despite being more expensive and giving away a three-year head start. It is also interesting to see that the Grand's sales haven't varied by that much throughout this 10-year period, whereas the Cherokee dived considerably in '97 (the drop caused by reduced stocks due to the change to a new model) and, after picking up in 1998, plunged even more so during the following three years as the new model was anticipated and the outgoing car started to look rather antiquated against its bigger brother.

VIN and engine numbers

All Cherokees were made with a unique Vehicle Identification Number (VIN) which has to be fitted somewhere on the vehicle. The VIN contains 17 characters that provide data concerning the vehicle. To protect the consumer from theft and possible fraud the manufacturer is required to include a Check Digit at the ninth position of the Vehicle Identification Number. The check digit is used by the manufacturer and government agencies to verify the authenticity of the vehicle and official documentation. The formula to use the check digit is not released to the general public. It has long been the practice to fit a stamped plate to the car, usually in the engine bay, but with theft methods getting ever more complex, later cars have the VIN stamped elsewhere, typically on the dashboard and visible through the windscreen from outside. When buying, it is absolutely essential that the VIN – wherever it is – shows no sign of being tampered with.

Cherokee XJ (1993–2001)

The VIN number is stamped on a plate which is riveted to the left-hand side of the bulkhead in the engine bay.

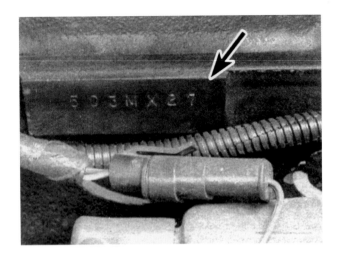

ENGINE NUMBERS

4.0L petrol
The number is stamped into a machined surface on the right-hand side of the block between number two and three cylinders.

2.5L petrol
The four-cylinder petrol engine has its engine number stamped into a machined surface on the right-hand side of the block between number three and four cylinders.

2.5L diesel
Stamped on the side of the left-hand side of the engine block on a machined flange.

Cherokee KJ (2001–onward)
The VIN number is fixed to the left-hand side 'A' pillar and is visible through the windscreen. The Vehicle Identification Number is also imprinted on the Vehicle Safety Certification Label and the frame rail.

ENGINE NUMBERS

2.4L petrol
Located on the rear of the cylinder block and virtually impossible to read without a ramp and a powerful lamp.

2.5 CRD diesel
Stamped on the side of the left-hand side of the engine block on a machined flange approximately halfway down the block.

3.7L petrol
Located at the right-front side of the engine block.

2.8 CRD diesel
The engine number is at the lower right-hand side of the block and is extremely difficult to see, even from underneath the vehicle.

VEHICLE SAFETY CERTIFICATION LABEL
A vehicle safety certification label certifies that the vehicle conforms to all applicable Federal Motor Vehicle Safety Standards. It also lists the month and year of vehicle manufacture, Gross Vehicle Weight Rating (GVWR). The gross front and rear axle weight ratings (GAWRs) are based on a minimum rim size and maximum cold tyre inflation pressure. This label also includes the Vehicle Identification Number (VIN), type of vehicle, type of rear wheels, Bar code, Month, Day and Hour (MDH) of final assembly, paint and trim codes and country of origin.

Grand Cherokee ZJ (1993–1999)

The VIN is stamped on a plate which is riveted to the left-hand side of the bulkhead in the engine bay.

Engine numbers are the same as those listed for Cherokee.

Grand Cherokee WJ (1999–onward)

The Vehicle Identification Number (VIN) plate is attached to the top-left side of the dashboard and is visible through the windscreen. The VIN contains 17 characters that provide data concerning the vehicle. Refer to the decoding chart to determine the identification of a vehicle.

VEHICLE SAFETY CERTIFICATION LABEL
This is on the shut face of the passenger side door, as with the Cherokee.

ENGINE NUMBERS
5.2L/5.9L petrol
The engine serial number is stamped on a machined pad located on the left-front corner of the cylinder block

4.7L petrol
Located at the right-front side of the engine block.

3.1 diesel
Stamped on the side of the left-hand side of the engine block on a machined flange approximately halfway down the block.

2.7L CRD diesel
The number is shown in two places. It can be stamped into a flat surface on the left-hand side of the engine bell housing close to the crankshaft sensor. You will also find it stamped on a flat surface above the left-hand side engine mounting bracket, and is very hard to see from above, as it is shielded by the manifold.

Appendix D

Useful contacts

As well as the postal address and telephone number for each company, the E-mail and Website address have also been included where available. If you are buying 'online', it is important to ensure that the site is 'secure' and that your credit card details cannot be stolen by a third party. In addition, we would not recommend any Internet connection or E-mail communication without some form of anti-virus protection to inhibit potentially dangerous computer 'bugs' getting into your machine and wreaking havoc. A personal 'firewall' should prevent computer hackers breaking into and entering your machine and stealing card and PIN numbers etc. All addresses and sites were correct at the time of writing, but are subject to change.

Autoleads, Unit 80, Woolmer Trading Estate, Bordon, Hants GU35 9QF. Tel: 01420 476767. E-mail: info@autoleads.co.uk. Website: www.autoleads.co.uk. All manner of ICE accessories and adaptors to make connecting new items of non-original sound equipment easy. Most products are available from Halfords.

Brightwells, Country Vehicle Auctions, A49 Bypass, Leominster, Herefordshire HR6 8NZ. Tel: 01568 611166. E-mail: vehicles@brightwells.com. Website: www.brightwells.com. Auctioneers with a regular 4x4 auction where you can usually find a selection of Jeep models.

Carflow. See Evo.

Car Parts Direct, 160 Burton Road, Derby DE1 1TN. Tel: 01332 290833. E-mail: sales@carparts-direct.co.uk. Website: www.carparts-direct.co.uk. All kinds of maintenance parts and accessories, including catalyst exhausts and Rossini drilled and grooved brake discs.

Clarke International, Hemnal Street, Epping, Essex CM16 4LG. Tel: 01992 565300. E-mail: clarkeint@aol.com. All kinds of hand tools and pneumatic machinery and tools, work benches, etc. See Machine Mart.

DaimlerChrysler UK Limited, Tongwell, Milton Keynes, Bucks MK15 8BA. Tel: 0800 616159 (off-road skills and events days 08456 447737). UK importers of all Jeep models. Website: www.jeep.co.uk.

DaimlerChrysler (USA HQ), 1000 Chrysler Drive, Auburn Hills, Michigan, USA 48326-2766. Tel: +1 248 512 2694. Jeep manufacturer.

Department of Transport (DETR), Public Enquiries Unit. Tel: 0207 890 3333. All matters relating to vehicle/roads legislation and the environment.

EDM Jeep Specialists, Unit 7, Field Farm Business Centre, Near Launton, Bicester, Oxon OX26 5EL. Tel: 01869 278942. Website: www.edm-jeep.co.uk. Specialist in the routine servicing and repair of Jeep vehicles of all ages. Supply and fitment of suspension lift kits, off-road equipment, accessories, tow bars and tyres. A well-stocked parts department with next-day mail order service on common parts. Courtesy cars available.

Equicar Ltd, Meadow Lane, Coseley, Wolverhampton, West Midlands WV14 9NQ. Tel: 01902 882 883. E-mail: Sales@equicar4x4.co.uk. Website: www.equicar.co.uk. Specialist dismantlers of 4x4 vehicles, an ideal starting place for locating expensive (new) or hard-to-find parts.

Evo Automotive Solutions, Unit 7, Denbigh Hall, Milton Keynes, Bucks MK3 7QT. Tel: 01908 646566. Suppliers of top quality Evo/Carflow locking wheel bolts to suit Jeep steel or alloy wheels.

Explorer UK, Poplar Park, Cliff Lane, Lymm, Cheshire WA13 0TD. Tel: 01925 757588. Website:

www.explorerprocomp.co.uk. Uprated suspensions specialists for all Jeep models.

Finlay, Gordon, Woolcombes, Newton Poppleford, Sidmouth, Devon EX10 0DF. Tel: 01395 567046. E-mail: sales@gordonfinlay-lpgconversions. Website: www.gordonfinlay-lpgconversions.co.uk. LPG conversion specialists (See also Iwema Enterprise.)

Garmin (Europe) Ltd, Unit 5, The Quadrangle, Abbey Park, Romsey, Hants SO51 9AQ. Tel: 01794 519944. Website: www.garmin.com. Producers of a whole range of portable satellite navigation devices, ideal for the Jeep owner, whether going off into the wilderness or delving the depths of Deptford.

Global Positioning Systems, Roseberry Court, Ellerbeck Way, Stokesley Business Park, Teesside TS9 5QT. E-mail: customerservices@globalpositioningsystems. co.uk. Website: www.globalpositioningsystems.co.uk. A wide range of GPS products and services, including Garmin and Magellan products.

Goodyear Great Britain Ltd, Stafford Road, Wolverhampton, West Midlands WV10 6DH. Tel: 01902 327000. Website: www.goodyear.co.uk. Wide range of quality on-road/off-road/in-between tyres and quite suitably, an American-based company.

Iwema Enterprise, Duinbeek 3, 5653PL Eindhoven, Holland. Tel: 0(031) 40 252 3950. E-mail: iwema.lpg@chello.nl. Website: www.iwemaenterprise.nl/. LPG conversions specialists, with a wide range of kits and components for all Jeep models including diesel. (See also Gordon Finlay.)

Machine Mart, 211 Lower Parliament Street, Nottingham NG1 1GN. Tel: 0870 770 7800. E-mail: sales@machinemart.co.uk. Website: www.machinemart.co.uk. Retail outlet for Clarke hand and machine tools.

M.A.D. Suspension, Comptek Ltd, Yorks Farm Business Centre, Towcester, Northants NN12 8EU. Tel: 01327 831313. E-mail: info@mad-suspension.co.uk. Website: www.mad-suspension.co.uk. The interactive suspension airbag system which utilises an on-board pneumatic pump to raise and lower rear coil springs to compensate for extra loads and/or large trailer weights.

Magellan. Website: www.magellangps.com. A wide range of portable GPS systems. See Global Positioning Systems for UK sales.

McGard, Smarter Direct Marketing Ltd, Parsonage Farm, Penn, Bucks HP10 8PE. Tel: 01494 817080, E-mail: info@smarterdirect.com. Website:

www.mcgard.com. Manufacturers of excellent quality, award-winning Ultra High Security locking wheel nuts suitable for both alloy and steel wheels.

MetaSystem UK Ltd, Oakmore Court, Kingswood Road, Hampton Lovett, Droitwich, Worcs WR9 0QH. Tel: 01905 791700. E-mail: info@metasystem.co.uk. Website: www.metaystem.co.uk. Automotive security specialists, with many aftermarket alarms and immobilisers, plus the Targa number-plate reversing aid.

Off Road MDG, 73–75 Clarence Street, Portsmouth, Hants PO1 4AY. Tel: 02392 755412. E-mail: Sales@offroadmdg.com. Website: www.offroadmdg.com. Jeep specialist, whether for servicing or repairs, axles overhauling, off-road preparation or a complete project vehicle build.

Raceways, Unit 6, The Maltings, Derby Road, Burton-on-Trent, Staffs DE14 1RN. Tel: 01283 517935. Website: www.raceways.co.uk. Specialists in American wheels and Cooper tyres for road, off-road or in-between.

Roof Box Company, The, Unit 1A, Toll Bar Estate, Sedbergh, Cumbria LA10 5HA. Tel: 08700 766326. E-mail: enquiries@roofbox.co.uk. Website: www.roofbox.co.uk. Range of roof boxes, cycle carriers, boot liners and Walser waterproof seat covers, all ideal for the Jeep enthusiast wanting to get away from it all and getting messy in the process.

SIP (Industrial Products Ltd), Gelders Hall Road, Shepshed, Loughborough, Leics LE12 9NH. Tel: 01509 503141. E-mail: info@sip-group.com. Website: www.sip-group.com. High-quality DIY/professional welding equipment, portable generators and air tools.

SmarTire Europe Ltd, Park 34, Didcot, Oxfordshire OX11 7WB. E-mail: info@smartire.co.uk. Website: www.smartire.com. Electronic pressure checking/warning system which works from inside the car and gives pressure and temperature warnings, even when the vehicle is moving.

Specialist Leisure Ltd, Unit D2, Taylor Business Park, Risley, Warrington, Cheshire WA3 6BH. E-mail: Info@specialist-leisure.co.uk. Website: www.specialist-leisure.co.uk. Wide range of aftermarket accessories for your Jeep, including lamps, winches, wheels and tyres, batteries and suspension.

Surrey Off-Road Specialists Ltd, Alfold Road, Dunsfold, Surrey GU8 4NP. Tel: 01483 200046. E-mail: upgrade@surreyoff-road.com. Website:

www.surreyoff-road.com. Wide range of aftermarket accessories for your Jeep, including GKN Driveline, ARB diff lockers, Optima batteries, Old Man Emu suspension. Also servicing, event preparation, audio, lights etc.

Teng Tools (Toolstars UK), Unit 5, Flitwick Industrial Estate, Maulden Road, Flitwick, Beds MK45 1UF. Tel: 01525 718080. E-mail: sales@toolstars.co.uk. Website: www.tengtools.co.uk. Importers of Teng's range of high-quality hand tools.

Thatcham, Colthrop Lane, Thatcham, Newbury, Berks RG19 4NP. Tel: 01635 868855. E-mail: enquiries@thatcham.org. Website: www.thatcham.org. The insurance industry testing body. The fitting of an approved device helps safeguard your Cherokee and can lead to insurance discounts.

van Aaken Developments Ltd., Crowthorne Business Centre, Telford Avenue, Crowthorne, Berks RG45 6XA. Tel: 01344 777553. E-mail: vanaaken@vanaaken.com. Website: www.vanaaken.com. Electronic tuning for petrol and diesel engines using 'Smart' chips and 'black box' technology.

VSIB (Vehicle Security Installation Board), Bates Business Centre, Church Road, Harold Wood, Romford, Essex RM3 0JF. Tel: 01708 340911. E-mail: E-mail@vsib.co.uk. Website: www.vsib.co.uk. The National Regulatory and Accreditation body for Vehicle Systems Installers and their installations.

Wakefield Storage Handling Ltd, Radford Road, New Basford, Nottingham NG7 7EF. Tel: 0115 854 1000. Importers of top-quality, Equipto benches and workshop storage equipment.

The Walnut Dash Company, 17 Church Road, Great Bookham, Leatherhead, Surrey KT23 3PG. Tel: 01372 451659. E-mail: sales@walnutdash.fsnet.co.uk. Website: www.walnutdash.fsnet.co.uk. Suppliers of high-quality, self-adhesive precision-cut walnut interior trim complete with a 10-year warranty. Also repairers of existing wooden trim.

Westbury Jeep, Featherbed Lane, Shrewsbury, Shropshire SY1 4NU. Tel: 01743 441445. E-mail: service@westburyonline.co.uk. Website: www.westburyonline.co.uk. Official DaimlerChrysler Jeep dealership, instrumental in the production of this book.

Specialist magazines

Jeep World, Kelsey Publishing Group, Cudham Tithe Barn, Berry's Hill, Cudham, Kent TN16 3AG. Tel: 01959 541444. E-mail: jeep.info@kelsey.co.uk. Website: www.kelsey.co.uk. Monthly Jeep magazine, from Second World War to latest Grand Cherokee. Includes classified ads, Jeep directory, discounted insurance, huge book shop.

4x4 Magazine (formerly *Off Road and 4-wheel Drive*), PO Box 106, Croydon, Surrey CR9 2TA. Tel: 0208 774 0600. Website: www.ipcmedia.com.

Clubs and organisations

Jeep Club UK, Website: www.jeepclub.co.uk. An enthusiastic club for owners of all Jeep models. Lots of events going on throughout the year and some great classified ads. It also arranges comprehensive off-road training days with experienced dealers.

Jeep Adventure Club, Website: www.j33p.org. The club is aimed at intermediate and advanced off-roaders with a focus on Jeep-branded vehicles. Membership allows you to contribute to the message board, and membership is free of charge.

Jeepey.co.uk, Andy and Mike Bonner. Tel: 01482 669123. E-mail: andybonner125@yahoo.co.uk. Website: www.jeepey.co.uk. A club which organises off-road gatherings, trials, green lane runs, shows, pub meets etc., with a local off road course available. Free membership with meetings on the third Wednesday of the month at the Percy Arms, High Street, Airmyn Goole DN14 8LD.

Index